Fourth edition

New Headway

Upper-Intermediate Workbook with key

John and Liz Soars
Jo McCaul

with **iChecker** CD-ROM

Assess › Progress

OXFORD
UNIVERSITY PRESS

Contents

See **iChecker** CD-ROM for **AUDIO BANK**, **UNIT TESTS**, and **LINKS**

3001542
£1650

1

The tense system • *have/have got* • Compound nouns
• Phrasal verbs – literal and idomatic • Sounds and spelling

Home and away!

The tense system

1 Identifying tenses

1 Write the correct verb form, active or passive, using the verb in the box.

walk

1 **A** How did you get here?

B We **walked** . It didn't take long.

2 'Hello Mary? It's me. Listen, I _____ just _____ up your road – I'll be with you in five minutes!'

3 I need to sit down. We _____ for hours.

take

4 It was a hard match. At half-time, one of the footballers _____ to hospital.

5 This shirt fits me perfectly. I _____ it.

6 My dog looked guilty. He _____ some food from the kitchen table.

have

7 We need a new car. We _____ this one for ages.

8 We _____ a lovely picnic until my wife was stung by a bee.

9 Don't phone at 8.00. We _____ dinner then.

make

10 Our sandwiches _____ freshly _____ daily.

11 Have you heard about Lenny? He _____ redundant.

12 By the time I'm 40, I _____ enough money to retire.

wash

13 **A** Where are my jeans?

B They _____ at the moment.

14 My favourite white T-shirt went pink. It _____ with my daughter's red jumper.

15 Simon was all wet because he _____ the car.

sell

16 My sister _____ her home-made cakes at the market on Saturdays.

17 If no one offers to buy the house, it _____ by auction next month.

18 I wish I'd bought that antique chair I saw. I'm sure it **will have been sold** by now.

teach

19 At the end of this term, I _____ for six years.

20 The children _____ how to make cakes when one boy dropped his bowl on the teacher's foot.

2 Complete the chart with the verb forms from exercise 1.

Active	Simple	Continuous
Present		
Past	walked	
Future		
Present perfect		
Past Perfect		
Future Perfect		
Passive	**Simple**	**Continuous**
Present		
Past		
Future		
Present Perfect		
Past Perfect		
Future Perfect	will have been sold	

2 Check it

Correct the sentences.

I'm working
1 ~~I work~~ ∧ hard at the moment because I have exams next week.
2 It's really cold lately, so I've bought a new winter coat.
3 Manchester United play really well at the moment. Their new player has real talent.
4 I've heard you are passing all your exams. Congratulations!
5 I was doing my homework when my friend was calling.
6 When I was a little girl, I've always spent my pocket money on sweets.
7 I went out with Paulo for two years now, and we're still crazy about each other.
8 I can't decide what to buy my brother for his birthday. Perhaps I'm going to get him a new shirt.
9 A one-day strike has called by French air traffic control for this Friday.
10 The teacher said that Megan had been working hard and was deserved to pass all her exams.

3 Using the correct tense

Read the Skype conversation between Nicola in Australia and her parents in Britain. Put the verbs into the correct tense.

SKYPING THE FOLKS

N Hello! Dad, I ¹ _____ (look) at the top of your head at the moment! Reposition the camera so I can see your face.

D Sorry, I just ² _____ (not understand) this technology. I ³ _____ only just _____ (learn) how to text! Oh my! I can't believe it. I can see you on my computer screen Nicola! I ⁴ _____ (call) your mum. Jackie, come here quick!

N Dad, you're so funny. I ⁵ _____ (do) this for ages with my friends. It's so good to see your face. I ⁶ _____ (not see) you for so long!

D How are the children? They look so grown up in those photos you ⁷ _____ (email) us.

N They're fine. Ollie ⁸ _____ (study) for his Year 12 Certificate. He hopes he ⁹ _____ (accept) at the University of Melbourne next year. Becky ¹⁰ _____ (choose) to play for her university netball team – she's so pleased. Anyway, how are you and Mum? Where is she? I want to speak to her.

D She ¹¹ _____ (get) a bit deaf. I ¹² _____ (shout) louder. Jackie, come here! It's Nicola. Anyway, where was I? We're both fine. We ¹³ _____ (go) on holiday last month but we just ¹⁴ _____ (stay) at a cheap bed and breakfast

in Brighton to get some sea air. We ¹⁵ _____ (save) hard at the moment to come and see you at Christmas. I ¹⁶ _____ (not realize) how expensive flights are. At last! Here's your mum. Jackie, what ¹⁷ _____ you _____ (do)?

M Sorry, I ¹⁸ _____ (not hear) you. Oh my! It's our Nicola on the computer, as clear as can be. Hi, darling! I wish I could give you a big hug.

N Me too, Mum. Not long now before you and Dad ¹⁹ _____ (be) here. At least now we can see each other. Now you know what to do, we can Skype every weekend.

M Lovely, we ²⁰ _____ (look forward to) that. Anyway, tell us how you are, darling ...

🎧 Listen and check.

Passives

4 Active or passive?

1 These active sentences can sound unnatural. Rewrite them using the passive.

1 They built our house in the 17th century.

_____ .

2 Someone's decorating my flat at the moment.

_____ .

3 Has someone fixed the coffee machine yet?

_____ ?

4 We ate in restaurants while they were building the new kitchen.
While the new kitchen _____

_____ .

5 When we went up to our hotel room, we found that someone hadn't cleaned it.

_____ .

6 They won't recognize her in those dark glasses.
She _____ .

2 Put the verbs in brackets into the correct tense and form, active or passive.

1 The burglars _____ (catch) as they _____ (leave) the office.

2 The postbox _____ always _____ (empty) at 12 noon.

3 Her neighbours _____ (grant) permission to build a huge extension.

4 We _____ (drive) down a quiet country lane when suddenly we _____ (overtake) by a police car.

5 When I woke up this morning, the world looked magical. It _____ (snow) all night.

6 When you _____ (arrive) in New York, you _____ (pick up) by one of our drivers and taken to the conference centre.

5 Tense review

1 Put the verbs into the correct tense, active or passive, positive or negative.

Living abroad

My name is Matt Perry and I'm 14 years old. My family
[1] _____ (move) to Japan from Denver, Colorado three years ago, and we [2] _____ (live) in Tokyo for the past two years. At first it was a real culture shock and I
[3] _____ (think) I'd never fit in, but now Tokyo feels just like home, and I [4] _____ (miss) it when we go back to Denver next year.

Why did we move?

My dad's an officer in the US Air Force and he [5] _____ (be/relocate) to work in other countries several times. In the past, Mum and I stayed in Denver, but we [6] _____ (not want) to be apart from my dad again, so this time we all moved. We [7] _____ (be) here for four years by the time we return home. That's the longest my dad
[8] _____ (live) anywhere since he was my age.

2 Here are the answers to some questions about Matt. Complete the questions.

1 How _____ ?
For three years.

2 Where _____ ?
Denver, Colorado.

3 Why _____ ?
His father was relocated there.

4 What _____ ?
He joined a football club.

5 What _____ for three years?
Japanese.

6 Why _____ ?
Because the characters are confusing.

7 What _____ ?
TV and comics.

8 When _____ ?
Next year.

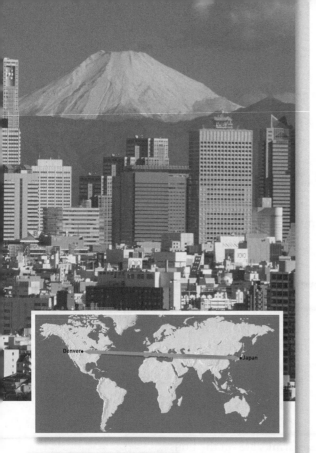

What's it like in Japan?

I [9] _____ always _____ (think) that Japanese people were quite reserved, but they're really sociable. When we first arrived, I [10] _____ (join) a football club and I [11] _____ (make) lots of American, English, and Japanese friends. I [12] _____ (learn) the language for three years now and my Japanese friends say I'm pretty good. But I [13] _____ (not like) writing Japanese because I always [14] _____ (get) confused by the characters.

What do I miss most?

I miss the TV and my comics, though it [15] _____ (get) better all the time. Soon I [16] _____ (be able to) buy my favourite American comic here. I also miss basketball, which was my favourite sport before we came to Japan. My mum [17] _____ (miss) her garden because we [18] _____ (not live) in a house, but a fourth-floor apartment. Anyway, we [19] _____ (be) back in Denver next year and I'm sure we [20] _____ all _____ (miss) so many things about Japan.

I know I'm only 14, but I've learned an awful lot about myself from living abroad. I'm going to feel very grown up compared to the other kids when I get home.

Auxiliary verbs

6 *have*, *be*, or *do*?

Complete the sentences with the correct form of *have*, *be*, or *do*. Write **A** for an auxiliary verb and **F** for a full verb. Sometimes the auxiliary is negative.

1 [A] They _had_ finished supper when we arrived.
2 [F] We _didn't have_ pizza for supper last night.
3 ☐ It _____ been a lovely day. Thank you.
4 ☐ I always _____ a shower after work.
5 ☐ I _____ always had a passion for Indian food.
6 ☐ Maria overslept, so she _____ catch her train.
7 ☐ What have you _____ to your hair? You look awful!
8 ☐ What _____ your new boyfriend look like?
9 ☐ This graffiti _____ done by British artist Banksy.
10 ☐ My boiler _____ being repaired at the moment.
11 ☐ I hate _____ the washing-up. I'd like a dishwasher.
12 ☐ I _____ my homework very quickly last night.

have or *have got*?

7 Forms of *have* and *have got*

Complete the conversations with a form of *have* or *have got*. Sometimes both forms are possible.

1 **A** Rebecca, _____ you _____ a headache?
   B Yes, I _____ difficulty sleeping at the moment.
   A Oh dear. Why is that?
   B Oh, the usual money worries. _____ you _____ an aspirin?

2 **A** _____ you _____ any pets?
   B No, we _____ . _____ you?
   A Oh yes. I _____ pets all my life. At the moment, I _____ a dog, two cats, and two mice.
   B I'd love _____ a dog, but I'm not so sure about mice!

3 **A** Come on! We _____ to hurry. We're late!
   B But I _____ my passport. I can't find it anywhere!
   A You _____ it yesterday. _____ a look in your bag.
   B I _____ it! You were right.

4 **A** I'm looking forward to _____ a few days' holiday. I _____ so much work for the past couple of months. I _____ a break for ages.
   B You're lucky! I _____ any holiday left!

Vocabulary

8 Compound nouns

Write one word to make three compound nouns. Check the use of hyphens, one word, or two words in your dictionary.

1 ☐ test / pressure / donor

2 ☐ worm / shelf / cover

3 ☐ fall / melon / skiing

4 ☐ fingers / house / salad

5 ☐ club / mare / time

6 brief / suit / book ☐

7 tea / make-up / plastic ☐

8 ☐ bow / coat / drop

9 ☐ shine / rise / set

10 ☐ works / sign / map

11 ☐ line / conditioning / fare

12 ☐ light / break / dream

13 ☐ shake / writing / bag

14 ☐ cube / berg / rink

15 ☐ scape / lady / slide

16 birthday / credit / business ☐

17 ☐ car / man / wear

18 note / address / visitors' ☐

9 *house* and *home* idioms

1 Tick (✓) the correct definition for each idiom. Use your dictionary.

1 They get on like a house on fire.
   a ☐ They have a very good relationship.
   b ☐ They are always arguing.

2 Come in and make yourself at home.
   a ☐ Tidy the house.
   b ☐ Please behave in my house as if it were yours.

3 Lloyd Webber's new musical brought the house down.
   a ☐ The musical was a success.
   b ☐ The musical wasn't a success.

4 The news report really brought home to me the horrors of famine.
   a ☐ The report talked about the horrors of famine.
   b ☐ The report made me realize fully the horrors of the famine.

5 These drinks are on the house.
   a ☐ These drinks are very pricey.
   b ☐ These drinks are free of charge.

6 This shaky old bridge is actually (as) safe as houses.
   a ☐ Don't worry. The bridge is very safe.
   b ☐ Be careful. The bridge isn't safe at all.

2 Complete the conversations with the idioms from exercise 1 in the correct form.

1 A I was so sorry to hear that your cat died.
   B Thank you. When I saw her empty bowl, it really _____ the fact that I'd never see her again.

2 A How did the meeting with Andy's parents go?
   B It was great. We all _____ _____ .

3 A Hello! Sorry we're so late. The traffic was terrible.
   B Don't worry. Just sit down and _____ _____ ! I'll put the kettle on.

4 A Did you read those excellent reviews in the local paper about the school play?
   B Yes, I did. Apparently, it _____ _____ !

5 A I'm not going up there. It looks a bit dangerous!
   B Oh, come on! It's _____ , and the view from the top is fantastic!

6 A How was that new restaurant you went to?
   B Well, the food was overpriced, but the manager gave us champagne _____ _____ because it was my birthday!

Phrasal verbs

10 Literal and idiomatic meanings

Phrasal verbs sometimes have a literal meaning, and sometimes an idiomatic meaning:

*Look Mum! My tooth's **fallen out**.* (literal)

*Jenny and Joe **have fallen out** again.* (idiomatic)

Literal

1 Complete the sentences with a particle from the box. Some are used more than once.

> away   on   off   back   out   down   in

1 The dentist said my tooth was bad. He had to pull it _____ .

2 Don't run _____ ! Come here! I want to talk to you.

3 My aunt fell _____ the stairs and broke her leg.

4 I fell _____ my horse!

5 When the sun went _____ , it was really cold.

6 A button has come _____ my shirt. Could you sew it back _____ for me?

7 I don't feel like cooking tonight. Shall we eat _____ instead?

8 I'm going to the library to take _____ the books I've finished.

9 I've just hung the washing out, and it's starting to rain. Can you help me to bring it _____ ?

10 Don't throw the box _____ . I'm sure I can use it for something.

Literal or idiomatic?

2 Complete the pairs of sentences with the same phrasal verb from the box in the correct form. Write **L** for a literal meaning and **I** for an idiomatic one.

> take off   pick up   sort out   put up   stand up   hold on

1 ☐ I'm coming to London for an interview next week – can you _____ me _____ for the night?

☐ _____ your hand if you know the answer.

2 ☐ I _____ all my clothes drawers today, so now I know where everything is.

☐ We've got a problem here, but if we try hard, I'm sure we can _____ it _____ .

3 ☐ When I was at school, we had to _____ when the teacher came in the room.

☐ You shouldn't let your sister tell you what to do all the time. You should _____ for yourself more, and say what you think.

4 ☐ It's too warm to be wearing a jumper. Why don't you _____ it _____ ?

☐ After a slow start, my business finally started to _____ .

5 ☐ I was never taught how to cook. I just _____ it _____ from my mother.

☐ Can you please _____ the chocolate wrapper you have just dropped!

6 ☐ **A** Can I speak to Kate, please?
B _____ . I'll just get her.

☐ When you're riding on the back of a motorbike, you have to _____ tight.

Listening

11 Missing home

1 🎧 Listen to Nancy and Amy, two first-year university students, talking about living away from home. Tick (✓) the things they miss.

1 ☐ boyfriend

2 ☐ dad's chicken curry

3 ☐ friends from home

4 ☐ living in a house

5 ☐ being looked after by parents

6 ☐ family pet

2 🎧 Listen again. Mark the sentences true (✓) or false (✗).

1 ☐ Nancy's mum bought her a cake.

2 ☐ Nancy likes the chips in the canteen.

3 ☐ Nancy and Amy do lots of cooking.

4 ☐ Everyone else seems to be having a good time.

5 ☐ Nancy likes going out all the time.

6 ☐ The communal kitchen is very clean.

7 ☐ Amy likes being more independent.

3 Look at the tapescript on p83. Find examples of missing words in the conversation.

Pronunciation

12 Vowel sounds and spelling

1 🎧 Each of these words in phonetics has a different English vowel sound. Listen and write the words.

▶▶ **Phonetic symbols p100**

1	/frend/	_____	7	/fænz/	_____
2	/ˈɪŋglɪʃ/	_____	8	/bɒks/	_____
3	/kliːn/	_____	9	/θɔːt/	_____
4	/mʌnθ/	_____	10	/wɜːk/	_____
5	/tʊk/	_____	11	/tʃɑːt/	_____
6	/njuːz/	_____	12	/ˈwɪntə/	_____

2 Complete the chart with the words from the box. There are three words for each vowel sound.

~~letter~~	busy	water	woman
~~freak~~	dead	drew	suspicious
decide	alarm	business	drop
barrier	birth	adopt	culprit
sweeper	earth	lethal	abroad
beggar	far	orphanage	shelter
zoom	father	couple	autobiography
family	Sir	accident	shock
rough	should	goodness	suitable

/e/	/ɪ/	/iː/	/ʌ/
letter	_____	freak	_____
_____	_____	_____	_____
_____	_____	_____	_____

/ʊ/	/uː/	/æ/	/ɒ/
_____	_____	_____	_____
_____	_____	_____	_____
_____	_____	_____	_____

/ɔː/	/ɜː/	/ɑː/	/ə/
_____	_____	_____	_____
_____	_____	_____	_____
_____	_____	_____	_____

🎧 Listen and check.

2

Present Perfect • **Simple and continuous**
• *have something done* • **Travel and transport**
• **Prepositions of movement** • **Word stress**

Been there, got the T-shirt!

Simple or continuous verb forms?

1 Present Perfect Simple or Continuous?

Match the lines to make sentences.

A	B
1 a He's written b He's been writing	three magazine articles so far. a travel blog since he left home.
2 a They've missed b They've been missing	you lots, so come home soon. the bus again.
3 a Paula's been leaving b Paula's left	work early to run some errands. work early all this week.
4 a I've lost b I've been losing	weight recently. my car keys.
5 a She's been talking b She's talked	on the phone for ages. about this subject before.
6 a The cat's been going b The cat's gone	next door to have its dinner. upstairs.
7 a He's had b He's been having	a heart attack. second thoughts about the job.
8 a I've been saving up b I've saved up	to buy a brand new 52-inch TV. about £500.
9 a I've been swimming, b I've swum	20 lengths today. which is why my hair is wet.
10 a I've been finding b I've found	my cheque book at last. it hard to concentrate recently.

2 Turning mountains of rubbish into gold.

Read the article and (circle) the correct verb form.

Turning mountains of **rubbish** into **gold**

Mount Everest is the highest mountain in the world, but unfortunately it is one of the messiest, too. Nearly 4,000 people [1] *have climbed / have been climbing* the 29,035-feet Mount Everest since the New Zealander Sir Edmund Hillary and Sherpa Tenzing first [2] *scaled / were scaling* its heights in 1953. But, unlike Hilary and Tenzing, these adventure tourists [3] *have dumped / have been dumping* tonnes of used equipment on Everest's slopes. Buried under snow in the winter, this junk is revealed in summer when the snow [4] *melts / is melting*.

However, now 15 Nepalese artists [5] *turn / are turning* the junk into art. They [6] *have worked / have been working* for a month to transform eight tonnes of Everest rubbish into 75 sculptures, which [7] *are now shown / are now being shown* at a hotel in the Nepalese capital, Kathmandu.

The rubbish used in the artworks [8] *was collected / was being collected* by Sherpa climbers. It [9] *includes / is including* old rope, tent poles, oxygen cylinders, drink cans, and even the remains of a helicopter. Kripa Rana Shahi, the project organizer, [10] *looked / was looking* for a way to spread awareness about keeping Everest clean when she [11] *had / was having* the ingenious idea of recycling the rubbish as works of art. She believes that Everest is Nepal's 'crown jewel'.

The sculptures [12] *range / are ranging* in price from $15 to $2,300. A percentage of the money [13] *will have gone / will be going* to the artist and the rest to the Everest Summiteers Association (ESA).

'Garbage on Everest is shameful.' says ESA chief, Wangchu Sherpa. 'We [14] *try / are trying* to turn it into gold here.'

Tortoise created out of discarded oxygen cylinder.

Mount Everest's rubbish turned into an art exhibition.

3 Present Perfect and Past Simple

Look at the Wallenda family's history. Complete the questions and answers.

The Flying Wallendas
Seven generations of performers

1700s	The Wallenda family began their career as circus performers.
Late 1800s	The Wallendas were known throughout Europe as the masters of the flying trapeze.
1920	Karl Wallenda first walked the tightrope without a net.
1928	All the Wallendas performed at Madison Square Garden where they walked the tightrope without a net after it was lost in shipping.
1944	The whole family fell off the tightrope in Ohio and survived. Thereafter, they became known as The Flying Wallendas.
1962	Two family members died when a seven-person pyramid went tragically wrong.
1963	Karl's sister-in-law, Rietta, fell to her death aged 43.
1978	Karl died after falling from a tightrope strung between two hotels in Puerto Rico. He was 73.
1979	Nik Wallenda was born in Sarasota, Florida.
1985	Nik decided he would walk a tightrope over the Niagara Falls one day – he was only six years old!
2001	The Flying Wallendas set a Guinness World Record with the first ever eight-person pyramid.
2012	Nik Wallenda fulfilled his childhood dream by walking a tightrope across the Niagara Falls.
2013	Nik Wallenda completed a quarter-mile-long tightrope walk, 1,500 feet over the Grand Canyon.

1 How long have the Wallenda family been performing?
Since _____ .

2 What _____ the Wallendas _____ as in the late 1800s?
The masters of the flying trapeze.

3 Why _____ the Wallendas _____
without a net?
Because they lost it in shipping.

4 What _____ to the whole family in Ohio?
They _____

_____ .

5 How long _____ they _____ The Flying Wallendas?
_____ 1944.

6 _____ Rietta when she _____ to her death?
Only 43.

7 Where and when _____ Nik _____ ?
In Sarasota _____ .

Simple or continuous review

4 Niagara daredevil

1 Read the news article and (circle) the correct verb form.

Friday June 15

NIAGARA DAREDEVIL

Tomorrow will be a historic day if Nik Wallenda [1] *becomes / is becoming* the first person in more than a century to cross the Niagara Falls from the US to Canada on a tightrope.

For nearly 30 years, Wallenda [2] *has tried / has been trying* to persuade the Niagara Parks Commission in Canada to let him walk across the Falls. At last, he [3] *has granted / has been granted* permission for the stunt to take place.

Daredevil Nik is a member of The Flying Wallendas, a family of circus performers spanning seven generations, who already [4] *holds / is holding* six Guinness World Records. He [5] *started / was starting* tightrope walking at the age of two and now has over 30 years' experience.

To prepare for the event, a team of firefighters ⁶ *were spraying / have been spraying* gallons of water at high pressure to replicate the power of spray from the Falls. Also, he ⁷ *has blasted / has been blasted* by a wind machine with gusts of up to 44 miles per hour. As Nik says, ⁸ 'We play / We're playing* with Mother Nature and Mother Nature has a mind of her own.'

Nik ⁹ *traverses / will be traversing* a 1,500-foot tightrope, which ¹⁰ *will be suspending / will be suspended* 200 feet above the roaring Falls. He says he loves the sensation of peace and calm that he ¹¹ *feels / is feeling* in the plumes of mist from the surging water.

Unbelievably, Nik ¹² *didn't want / wasn't wanting* to wear a safety harness, but ABC TV, who ¹³ *broadcast / are broadcasting* the event, would not risk the possibility of a man falling to his death ¹⁴ *showing / being shown* on live TV.

2 Complete the sentences. Use each verb twice, once in a simple and once in a continuous tense, active or passive.

1 rain

It **was raining** quite heavily when Nik Wallenda crossed the Niagara Falls on his tightrope.
It **rained** for days and our road was flooded.

2 perform

Cirque du Soleil _____ at the Royal Albert Hall since November.
David _____ so well in his school play that he got a standing ovation.

3 have

I _____ dinner with friends tonight.
They _____ three children, two boys and a girl.

4 think

You look worried. What _____ about?
I _____ it's time you had a haircut.

5 bang

I couldn't sleep because the garden gate _____ in the wind all night!
Ouch! I _____ just _____ my head on the cupboard door.

6 read

I _____ this book since the summer and I still haven't finished it!
I was thrilled when I _____ your email. What wonderful news!

7 fight

I _____ long and hard for my pay rise.
Where did you get that black eye from? _____ with your brother again?

8 expect

Could you get off the phone? I _____ a call.
I _____ you are studying hard for your exams at the moment.

9 decorate

Helen's house _____ at the moment so she's staying with a friend.
Their house _____ in a minimalist style.

10 lose

I think I must _____ my mind. I can't even remember what we did last weekend.
Kate is going on her honeymoon next week and she _____ her passport!

Passive

5 Present Perfect passive

1 Rewrite the sentences using the passive and omitting the subject.

1 The bin men have already collected the rubbish.

The rubbish **has already been collected.**

2 Have the workmen repaired the street lights yet?

_____ ?

3 The government has just passed some new anti-drug laws.

Some new anti-drug laws _____ .

4 The local council hasn't built any new homes for 20 years.

No _____ .

5 Nobody has watered the plants.

The plants _____ .

2 Rewrite the headlines using the Present Perfect passive.

1 **Rat Alert at Buckingham Palace**
Rats have been found at Buckingham Palace.

2 **Banker Bonuses Slashed**
_____ .

3 **Dramatic Rescue of Fishermen in Pacific**
_____ .

4 **Monsoon Kills over 400 in Pakistan**
_____ .

5 **Theft of Dali Painting in New York**
_____ .

6 **Ancient Pyramids Discovered in Sudan**
_____ .

7 **Missing Teenager Alive**
_____ .

8 **Council Shock – 464 Jobs Axed!**
_____ .

6 have something done

1 Look at the difference in meaning between these sentences:
I've repaired my bicycle. = I repaired it myself.
My bicycle has been repaired. = Someone repaired it. (The action is important, not who did it.)
I've had my bicycle repaired. = I arranged/paid for someone to repair it for me. (*have* + object + past participle)

2 *Have something done* is used to talk about services that you ask someone else to do.
*I'm going to **have my hair cut**.*

1 Rewrite the sentences using *have something done*.

1 John's kitchen is being decorated.

He's having his kitchen decorated.

2 My sister wants someone to pierce her ears.

She wants to _____ .

3 My eyes are going to be tested.

I'm going to _____ .

4 Mr and Mrs Turner's car has been serviced.

They _____ .

5 Our television hasn't been repaired yet.

We haven't _____ .

2 It's Melanie and Ken's wedding day. Look at the notes and write sentences about what they *have had / are having done*.

They've had the invitations printed.

She ...

He ...

Recently	– the invitations printed – wedding dress made – the cake decorated
Yesterday	– champagne delivered – hair cut
Today	– hair styled – flowers delivered
Next week	– photos developed – wedding dress and suit dry-cleaned

Listening

7 Off the beaten track

1 🎧 Listen to the radio programme. What do the three people do? Where did they visit?

Kay Morris

Vicky Smith

Gary Braithwaite

a _____ c _____ e _____

b _____ d _____ f _____

2 🎧 Listen again. Write **KM**, **VS** or **GB**. Who talks about … ?

1 an uninteresting hotel

2 a love of old western films

3 catching food to eat

4 the warm response they received from the local people

5 a sheltered childhood

6 a room with a beautiful view

3 Are the following statements true (✓) or false (✗)?

1 ☐ *Off the Beaten Track* is a radio programme that looks at different places to visit on holiday.

2 ☐ Kay has 13 years' experience in the travel business.

3 ☐ Vicky would prefer to stay in a hotel when she goes travelling from now on.

4 ☐ The Austrian hospice was much cheaper than the hotel.

5 ☐ When Gary first landed in America, he found it didn't live up to his childhood expectations.

6 ☐ The Navajo Nation feels like its part of the USA.

Vocabulary

4 The words below are all used in the listening. What collocations can you make by combining an adjective in **A** with a noun in **B**.

A	B
stunning	fire
friendly	terrace
romantic	welcome
enchanting	tourist
adventurous	views
sunlit	haunt
crackling	destination
interesting	places
enthusiastic	hotel
five-star	atmosphere
perfect	alternatives

Vocabulary

8 Travel and transport words

1 Tick the verbs which go with each form of transport.

	car	bus	bike	train	plane	ship/ferry
get into/out of						
get on/off						
take off						
land						
ride						
drive						
catch						
miss						
board						
park						

2 Complete the table below with the nouns in the box. Some can go into more than one column.

runway	platform	seat belt
helmet	harbour	carriage
traffic lights	life jacket	service station
season ticket	trolley	tyres
track	horn	port
one-way street	check-in desk	traffic jam
baggage rack	timetable	hand luggage
Customs	deck	traffic warden
cabin	aisle/window seat	cycle lane
security check	ticket inspector	overhead locker

car	bus	bike

train	plane	ship/ferry

Prepositions

9 Prepositions of movement

Complete the text with prepositions from the box.
Use each preposition at least once.

across	against	on	onto
along	in	off	into
up	out of	over	through
past	to	towards	at

Joe's journey across town

Joe's plane landed on time [1] _____ Heathrow airport. He had exactly one hour to get [2] _____ the airport and [3] _____ the centre of London to catch his train [4] _____ Manchester. He hurried [5] _____ customs and passport control, and then raced [6] _____ the taxi sign at the exit.

Unfortunately, at that moment, the strap on his rucksack broke and it fell [7] _____ his back and [8] _____ the ground. Dirty socks, shirts, and underpants spilled all [9] _____ the airport floor. Joe was so embarrassed! He stuffed everything back [10] _____ his rucksack and, pushing his way [11] _____ the crowds of people, finally made it [12] _____ the taxi rank. He jumped [13] _____ the nearest taxi, shouting 'Euston Station, quickly, please!' The taxi set off at such speed that Joe was thrown forward, hitting his face [14] _____ the glass partition. The taxi sped on and finally arrived [15] _____ the city centre, and inevitably, the middle of a traffic jam! It would be quicker to walk. Joe paid the driver, leapt [16] _____ the taxi and ran [17] _____ the pavement, [18] _____ all the brightly-lit shop windows. At last he could see the station opposite, but it was difficult to get [19] _____ the road because of all the traffic. He reached the station just as his train was leaving. He jumped [20] _____ the barrier, raced [21] _____ the platform, and leapt [22] _____ the train with seconds to spare. He sighed with relief – he would be home in time for Christmas.

Pronunciation

10 Word stress

1 Here are pairs of words in phonetic script. Look at the stress marks. Transcribe them.

▶▶ **Phonetic symbols p100**

1 /ɪkˈsplɔːrə/   /ekspləˈreɪʃn/

2 /ˈpɒlətɪks/   /ˌpɒləˈtɪʃn/

3 /ˈfəʊtəɡrɑːf/   /fəˈtɒɡrəfə/

4 /ˈlʌkʃəri/   /lʌɡˈʒʊəriəs/

5 /prəˈdjuːs/   /prəˈdʌkʃn/

6 /dʒəˈpæn/   /dʒæpəˈniːz/

🎧 Listen and practise saying them.

2 What is the stress pattern of the words in exercise 1? Write them in the chart.

● ●	● ● ●	● ● ●
	explorer	
● ● ●	● ● ● ●	● ● ● ●
	exploration	

3 Write the words in the box in the chart above.

instructor	destination	illegal
adrenaline	community	reject (v)
success	backpacker	Bangladesh
paradise	infinite	packaging
scientists	Philippines	charity
disappointment	European	pollute
spectacular	afternoon	complain
memorial	Cambodia	emergency
authentic		

🎧 Listen and practise saying them.

Narrative tenses • Time expressions
• Film, theatre, books • Phrasal verbs – type 1 • Diphthongs

News and views

Narrative tenses

1 Which narrative tense?

Complete the article with the verbs in the box. Use each verb once only.

Past Simple		Past Continuous	Past Perfect Simple	Past Perfect Continuous
saved	made	was drowning	had been	had been bodyboarding
hovered	was airlifted	was struggling	had arrived	
came through	was lowered	~~was piloting~~	had seen	
swept	were		had managed	
swam				

Prince William saves drowning girl

A heroic rescue

It has emerged that Prince William ¹ **was piloting** the Royal Air Force Sea King helicopter that ² _____ a teenage girl from drowning off the coast of Wales. He ³ _____ on duty for only 15 minutes when a call ⁴ _____ that a young girl ⁵ _____ in the sea. In less than a minute, the Prince and his crew ⁶ _____ at the scene.

Girls in distress!

Thirteen-year-old Tamara West ⁷ _____ when a rip tide ⁸ _____ her out to sea. From the beach, Tamara's older sister, Sharon, ⁹ _____ what had happened and ¹⁰ _____ out to save her. However, in the meantime, a surfer ¹¹ _____ to rescue Tamara, and it was now poor Sharon who ¹² _____ against the strong current and the waves.

Calm and controlled

Prince William calmly ¹³ _____ overhead in the Sea King whilst the paramedic, Master Aircrew Harry Harrison, ¹⁴ _____ to rescue the exhausted girl from the sea. The teenager ¹⁵ _____ to hospital where she ¹⁶ _____ a full recovery.

The Prince's superior officers ¹⁷ _____ full of praise for his handling of the sea rescue.

2 Irregular verbs

1 Complete the sentences with the irregular verb in either the Past Simple or the Past Perfect.

stick ☐

1 Becky _____ her tongue out at the teacher.

2 Someone _____ the exam results on the noticeboard earlier that morning.

fall ☐

3 Harry _____ in love with a Greek girl while he was working in Athens.

4 He _____ in love before, but this was different. He wanted to marry her.

cost ☐

5 It _____ an awful lot to have our car fixed.

6 Ted told me his new car _____ a fortune.

fly ☐

7 When I went to Australia, I was nervous because I _____ (never) before.

8 The plane took off and _____ into the clouds.

catch ☐

9 Suzy wondered how she _____ a cold in the middle of her summer holiday.

10 She _____ a taxi outside the restaurant, and went back to her hotel.

be ☐

11 Talks _____ held in New York last week to discuss global warming.

12 When the politicians left the talks, no decisions _____ reached.

2 Tick (✓) the verbs in exercise 1 which have the same form for the Past Simple and the past participle.

3 Past Simple or Past Continuous?

(Circle) the correct tense.

1 I *lived / was living* in Eastbourne when I *met / was meeting* my husband.

2 Our team *played / was playing* really well. We *won / were winning* at half time, but in the end we *lost / were losing* 3–2.

3 I *didn't think / wasn't thinking* of having a birthday party, but now I'm glad I *had / was having* one.

4 I'm so tired. The baby next door *was coughing / coughed* all night long and we *weren't getting / didn't get* any sleep.

5 It *was snowing / snowed* when I *got up / was getting up* this morning. The children next door *made / were making* a snowman, so I quickly *put / was putting* on some warm clothes and *raced / was racing* outside to help them.

6 James *was playing / played* happily when his big brother *hit / was hitting* him on the head and *made / was making* him cry.

7 A weird thing *happened / was happening* to me yesterday. I *was walking / walk* home when I *noticed / was noticing* a light hovering above me. I *wanted / was wanting* to get a photo, but it suddenly *vanished / was vanishing* into thin air.

8 Roger *sunbathed / was sunbathing* by the hotel pool when he *heard / was hearing* a strange sound. An enormous insect *appeared / was appearing* and *landed / was landing* on his leg.

4 Time expressions

1 Match the lines and time expressions. Use each expression once only.

1 [d] I've been working in the same bank	a ten years ago.
2 ☐ I started this job	b by the time I was 40.
3 ☐ I didn't want to get married	c until I was 30.
4 ☐ I had had two children	d for years.
5 ☐ I'd been writing poetry for years	e since six o'clock.
6 ☐ I didn't stay in that job	f until I arrived.
7 ☐ I've been waiting here	g when he finally arrived.
8 ☐ They didn't order the meal	h for long.
9 ☐ The train pulled out of the station	i a minute ago.
10 ☐ I'd been waiting over an hour	j until it was too late.
11 ☐ I haven't been feeling well	k until late.
12 ☐ They got on the plane	l lately.
13 ☐ I'd never seen him	m at the last minute.
14 ☐ I was watching TV	n before.
15 ☐ He didn't hear the attacker	o before being published.

2 Complete the sentences, using past tenses only and the prompts in brackets.

1 Two years ago, while I _____ .
   (work / Paris / grandfather / die)

2 As soon as I _____ .
   (get / home / switch on the TV)

3 First I _____ .
   (shower / then / get dressed)

4 Since I was a child, I _____ .
   (always / want / visit / Australia / finally / go / last year)

5 As he _____ .
   (post / letter / realize / not put on / stamp)

6 By the time he'd _____
   _____ . (finish / speak / most / audience / fall asleep)

7 Once I'd _____ .
   (tell him / truth / feel better)

8 Until I _____ .
   (find a flat / I / stay with friends / months)

Past passives

5 Active to passive

In these sentences the subject is either not important or too obvious to be necessary. Put each sentence into the passive.

1 Someone stole my bike last night.

   My bike was stolen last night.

2 Archaeologists discovered a Roman temple underneath the new housing estate.

   A Roman temple _____

   _____ .

3 The sports officials held the races indoors because it was raining.

   The races _____

   _____ .

4 Someone had booked the swimming pool for a children's party on Saturday afternoon.

   The swimming pool _____

   _____ .

5 The plumber was repairing the dishwasher, so I couldn't leave the house.

   The dishwasher _____

   _____ .

6 When we returned to our hotel room, the chambermaid still hadn't cleaned it.

   Our hotel room _____

   _____ .

7 The chef hadn't cooked the fish for long enough.

   The fish _____

   _____ .

8 Workmen were putting up new traffic lights at the crossroads.

   New traffic lights _____

   _____ .

Revision of active and passive

6 Film review

Read the review and complete it with a verb in the correct form.

MONSTERS UNIVERSITY

release	combine	show	adore	see

When I first ¹ _____ *Monsters, Inc.*, I loved it. Who didn't? In 2001, when the film ² _____ first _____ in cinemas, monsters Mike and Sulley ³ _____ by millions. Now, over a decade later, Pixar ⁴ _____ the prequel *Monsters University*. This is a movie that ⁵ _____ the humour from the first film with the latest animated technology to create one of Pixar's most exciting films to date!

loathe	study	become	overcome	tell	work	take

In *Monsters University*, we ⁶ _____ back in time to Mike and Sulley's student days before they ⁷ _____ for *Monsters, Inc.* They are 18 years old, and they ⁸ _____ at the Monstropolis University of Fear. We see how the two characters ⁹ _____ each other when they first meet, and this mutual hatred provides a great deal of humour. *Monsters University* ¹⁰ _____ the story of how Mike and Sulley ¹¹ _____ their differences and ¹² _____ the best of friends.

make	direct	compose	achieve	find	come

Dan Scanlon ¹³ _____ the film, Kori Rae produced it, and Randy Newman ¹⁴ _____ the music score. This is the first prequel that Pixar ¹⁵ _____ ever _____ . It was always going to be a challenge to recreate the magic of *Monsters, Inc.*, yet Pixar ¹⁶ _____ this with confidence and success. Technology ¹⁷ _____ a long way since 2001, and the computer animation is scarily realistic! The script is genius, and both parents and children ¹⁸ _____ it hilarious – a real family blockbuster.

Vocabulary

7 Film, theatre, books

Are the words connected with film (**F**), theatre (**T**), or books (**B**)? Some are connected with more than one.

act **F T**	director	e-reader	prequel/sequel	fairy tale	performance
plot	backstage	character	documentary	programme	thriller
storyline	trailer	musical	blockbuster	whodunnit	playwright
chapter	script	starring role	animation	science fiction	autobiography
stalls	rehearsal	novelist	screen	hardback	full house
critic	review	matinee	interval	dressing-room	paperback

Phrasal verbs

8 Type 1 – phrasal verbs with no object

There are four types of phrasal verb.

Type 1 phrasal verbs consist of a verb + adverb. There is no object.

They can be both literal and idiomatic.

She stood up and walked out. (literal)

The bomb went off. (idiomatic)

▶▶ **Type 2 and type 3 p36**   ▶▶ **Type 4 p48**

1 Match the phrasal verbs with their definitions.

1	find out	a	☐	have a more stable life
2	break up	b	☐	wait a minute
3	hold on	c	☐	be quiet
4	speak up	d	☑ 1	discover
5	set off	e	☐	be happier
6	stay in	f	☐	arrive
7	settle down	g	☐	talk louder
8	turn up	h	☐	not go out, stay at home
9	cheer up	i	☐	end a relationship
10	shut up	j	☐	begin a journey

2 Complete the sentences with the phrasal verbs from exercise 1 in the correct form.

1 Peter hasn't arrived yet – I hope he _____ soon.

2 We have a long journey tomorrow. What time are we _____ ?

3 Why are you so miserable? _____ !

4 I don't feel like going out tonight. Let's _____ and order a pizza?

5 Larry was a bit wild at university, but then he got a job, found a lovely wife, _____ and had kids.

6 After three years of going out together, Josh and Lil eventually _____ because Josh didn't want to get married.

7 Can I copy your homework? The teacher will never _____ .

8 _____ ! I'm trying to watch a programme and you're all talking.

9 _____ ! We can't hear you at the back!

10 **A** What's Bill's phone number?'

   B _____ ! I'll just look it up.

Listening

9 It's complicated!

1 🎧 Listen to a conversation between two friends, Julie and Amy. (Circle) the correct answer.

1 Last Sunday, Amy *had a relaxing afternoon* / *watched a film on TV*.

2 She wants to talk to Julie about *the film she watched* / *an article she's read*.

3 In the film, Meryl Streep is the ex-wife of *Steve Martin* / *Alec Baldwin*.

4 In the film, the husband yearns for *his ex-wife* / *a new, young wife*.

5 The article and the film have *the same* / *a different* message about divorce.

6 Linda and Graham had *an acrimonious* / *a civilized* divorce.

7 They are now *dating* / *living together* again.

2 🎧 Match lines in **A** and **B** for giving and responding to news.

A
1   I think it was called 'It's complicated'.
2   It reminded me of Linda and Graham.
3   Divorced couples can become friends.
4   They've started dating again.
5   You have to work hard at relationships.
6   I hope it works out for them.

B	
a ☐	They haven't! That's amazing.
b ☐	Yes, that was it.
c ☐	Did it? Why was that?
d ☐	Yes, me too.
e ☐	Actually, I can believe that.
f ☐	That's very true.

Pronunciation

10 Diphthongs

> Diphthongs are two vowel sounds which run together.
>
> **hear** /hɪə/ = /ɪ/ + /ə/ diphthong /ɪə/   **hair** /heə/ = /e/ + /ə/ diphthong /eə/
>
> ▶▶ Phonetic symbols p100

1 🎧 Listen and (circle) the correct transcription of each word. What is the other word? Read both aloud.

1 **pay**	/peɪ/ /peə/	3 **phone**	/fəʊn/ /faɪn/	5 **dear**	/dɪə/ /deə/	7 tour	/tʊə/ /təʊ/
2 **write**	/raɪt/ /raʊt/	4 **round**	/reɪnd/ /raʊnd/	6 **boy**	/bəʊ/ /bɔɪ/	8 fair	/fɪə/ /feə/

2 Read the poem aloud. Write the number next to the correct sound.

Sounds and letters don't agree

When the English tongue we speak,

Why does ¹ *break* not rhyme with ² *weak*?   **2** /iː/   **1** /eɪ/

Won't you tell me why it's true

We say ³ *sew*, but also ⁴ *few*? ☐ /uː/ ☐ /əʊ/

And the maker of a verse

Cannot rhyme his ⁵ *horse* with ⁶ *worse*? ☐ /ɔː/ ☐ /ɜː/

⁷ *Beard* is not the same as ⁸ *heard*. ☐ /ɜː/ ☐ /ɪə/

⁹ *Cord* is different from ¹⁰ *word*, ☐ /ɜː/ ☐ /ɔː/

¹¹ *Cow* is cow, but ¹² *low* is low, ☐ /aʊ/ ☐ /əʊ/

¹³ *Shoe* is never rhymed with ¹⁴ *foe*. ☐ /uː/ ☐ /əʊ/

Think of ¹⁵ *hose* and ¹⁶ *dose* and ¹⁷ *lose*, ☐ /uːz/ ☐ /əʊz/ ☐ /əʊs/

And think of ¹⁸ *loose* and yet of ¹⁹ *choose*, ☐ /uːz/ ☐ /uːs/

Think of ²⁰ *comb* and ²¹ *tomb* and ²² *bomb* ☐ /ɒm/ ☐ /uːm/ ☐ /əʊm/

²³ *Doll* and ²⁴ *roll* ☐ /ɒl/ ☐ /əʊl/

and ²⁵ *home* and ²⁶ *some*. ☐ /ʌm/ ☐ /əʊm/

And since ²⁷ *pay* is rhymed with ²⁸ *say* ☐ /eɪ/ ☐ /eɪ/

Why not ²⁹ *paid* with ³⁰ *said*, I pray? ☐ /eɪ/ ☐ /e/

Think of ³¹ *blood* and ³² *food* and ³³ *good*; ☐ /ʊ/ ☐ /uː/ ☐ /ʌ/

³⁴ *Mould* is not pronounced like ³⁵ *could*. ☐ /ʊd/ ☐ /əʊld/

Why is it ³⁶ *done*, but ³⁷ *gone* and ³⁸ *lone*? ☐ /əʊ/ ☐ /ʌ/ ☐ /ɒ/

Is there any reason known?

To sum up, it seems to me

That sounds and letters don't agree.

tomb

comb

bomb

🎧 Listen and check.

Questions • Negatives • Antonyms and synonyms
• Verb + preposition • Intonation in question tags

The naked truth

Questions

1 What's the question?

Read the text about Frank Abagnale and write questions for the answers.

1 __Why is Frank Abagnale__ one of the world's most famous impersonators?
Because he assumed at least eight identities, including a pilot and a doctor.

2 _____ was he a con man for?
Five years.

3 _____ ?
Stephen Spielberg.

4 _____ split up?
16.

5 _____ ?
Bank fraud.

6 _____ airline _____ con?
Pan Am.

7 _____ a paediatrician?
At a hospital in Georgia.

8 _____ ?
Because he nearly caused a baby to die!

9 _____ ?
Sociology.

10 _____ ?
In France.

11 _____ ?
Leonardo DiCaprio.

12 _____ ?
He works for the FBI.

The TRUE story of a REAL fake

Frank Abagnale is one of the world's most famous impersonators. During his life, he has assumed at least eight separate identities, including an airline pilot, a lawyer, a professor, and a doctor. He was also a brilliant conman who forged $2.5 million worth of cheques across 26 countries over the course of five years. Such was his fame that his adventures have been made into a Stephen Spielberg film and a Broadway musical, both called *Catch Me If You Can*.

Amazingly, Frank's career as a conman began when he was just 16. Upset at the divorce of his parents, he ran away to New York and, being tall, handsome, and already going grey, he pretended to be 26 and got a job. His first major con was bank fraud. He created a new identity and set up numerous bank accounts. He printed flawless fake cheques and managed to cash them at the banks.

However, Frank is most famous for impersonating an airline pilot. He conned Pan Am into giving him a pilot's uniform, and he faked an ID card. He was still only a teenager when he flew over 1,000,000 miles and visited 26 countries enjoying the glamorous lifestyle of an international pilot at Pan Am's expense!

dicaprio   hanks

catch me   if you can

The true story of a real fake.

Catch them in Cinemas

Frank also had the nerve to impersonate a paediatrician in a Georgia hospital and nearly caused a baby to die through oxygen deprivation. Having the sense to realize he was putting lives at risk, he changed course and became a university professor. He taught sociology and apparently his classes were very popular. By now, the police were on his trail, but he always managed to cover his tracks until eventually he was arrested in France and imprisoned for five years.

It is easy to understand how his amazing impersonations and adventures lent themselves to both a movie, starring Leonardo DiCaprio as Frank, and a highly successful Broadway musical.

Today, the majority of Frank's work is for the FBI, preventing fraud rather than committing it! He believes that fraud is too easy. 'Nowadays', he says, 'technology breeds crime' and 'prevention is the only feasible course of action'.

2 Indirect questions

1 Rewrite these questions using indirect forms.

1 How many identities did he have altogether?
I'm not sure exactly <u>how many identities he had.</u>

2 How did he learn to forge cheques?
I'd like to know _____ .

3 Why did his parents divorce?
I've no idea _____ .

4 Who decided to make a musical?
I wonder _____ .

5 Which countries did he visit?
I don't know _____ .

6 How did he have the nerve to impersonate a doctor?
I can't imagine _____ .

7 Why did the police take so long to catch him?
Do you know _____ ?

8 How did he get the job with the FBI?
I wish I knew _____ .

2 Write indirect questions about Frank Abagnale for these answers.

1 Have you any idea _____ ?
He made millions of dollars.

2 Can you tell me _____ ?
Catch Me If You Can.

3 I wonder _____ .
He flew for Pan Am.

4 Do you know _____ ?
Leonardo de Caprio and Tom Hanks starred in it.

5 Why do you think he _____ ?
Because he knows better than anyone how to prevent fraud.

3 Questions and prepositions

1 Complete the questions with the prepositions in the box.

in	of	by	with	to	from	at	about	~~for~~	on

1 What is your home town famous _for_ ?

2 Who was that book written _____ ?

3 Who does this dictionary belong _____ ?

4 What are you looking _____ ?

5 What did you spend all your money _____ ?

6 What sort of books are you interested _____ ?

7 What are you talking _____ ?

8 What are you so afraid _____ ?

9 Who are you angry _____ ? James or me?

10 **A** I got these flowers in the post today!

    B Ooh, they're beautiful! Who are they _____ ?

2 Write a short question with a preposition in reply to these sentences.

1 **A** I went to the cinema last night.

    B _Who with?_

2 **A** I'm very cross with you.

    B _____ ?

3 **A** We're going away for the weekend.

    B _____ ?

4 **A** I'm very worried.

    B _____ ?

5 **A** I'm going to Australia.

    B _____ ? Two weeks? A month?

6 **A** I bought a present today.

    B _____ ?

7 **A** Have you heard? Jane has got engaged.

    B _____ ?

8 **A** Can you cut this article out for me?

    B _____ ? I haven't got any scissors.

Negatives

4 Negative auxiliaries

Complete the sentences with the negative auxiliaries below.

isn't   weren't   hadn't   won't   aren't   hasn't   'm not   don't   doesn't   haven't   didn't   wasn't

1 My boss speaks fluent French, but I _____ .

2 We wanted to leave the party, but Fred _____ .

3 I've been to America, but my parents _____ .

4 I thought these biscuits were sugar-free, but they _____ .

5 They said she was getting better, but she _____ .

6 I'll be moving to London, but my girlfriend _____ .

7 My husband's going to the wedding, but I _____ .

8 Jo likes Indian food, but Andrew _____ .

9 Bill thought I'd forgotten our wedding anniversary, but I _____ .

10 The bedroom's been decorated, but the bathroom _____ .

11 He said that he was really sorry, but he _____ .

12 We thought that we were doing it correctly, but we _____ .

5 Negative questions

Match a question in **A** with a line in **B**.

A		B	
1	Don't you want me to help you?	a	I thought you did.
2	Do you want me to help you?	b	I will if you want.
3	Aren't you a member of the tennis club?	c	I'm sure I've seen you there.
4	Are you a member of the tennis club?	d	If you are, we could have a game.
5	Don't you know the answer?	e	Yes or no?
6	Do you know the answer?	f	I'm surprised at you!
7	Don't you think it's beautiful?	g	Surely you agree with me!
8	Do you think it's beautiful?	h	I'm asking because I'm not sure.
9	Didn't I tell you I'm going out tonight?	i	I can't remember now.
10	Did I tell you I'm going out tonight?	j	thought I had. Sorry!

6 *no*, *not*, *-n't*, or *none*?

Complete the sentences with *no*, *not*, *-n't*, or *none*.

1 I'll help you, but _____ tonight.

2 We have _____ onions left. Sorry!

3 _____ of us understood the lesson.

4 The teacher was _____ very clear.

5 I asked you _____ to make a mess.

6 Why did _____ you do what I asked?

7 How do you manage _____ to put on any weight?

8 Bring Alessia to the party, but _____ Ben. He's too loud.

9 There's _____ meat in this dish, so it's suitable for vegetarians.

10 **A** Who likes chemistry?

   B _____ me.

11 **A** Where's the nearest swimming pool?

   B There are _____ around here.

12 She has _____ idea of how to enjoy herself.

13 Why have _____ you emailed me for so long?

14 I can play the piano a little bit, but _____ properly.

15 **A** Do you work late?

   B _____ if I can help it.

16 **A** Where's the coffee?

   B There's _____ left.

17 The management accepts _____ responsibility for items left in the cloakroom.

18 I've got _____ time for people who are rude.

19 _____ of my friends smoke.

20 **A** Do you like jazz?

   B _____ usually.

"Didn't you get the e-mail?"

7 I don't think you're right

1 In English, we usually say *I don't think* + affirmative verb:
I **don't think I know** you.   NOT   ~~I think I don't~~ know you.
We do the same with *believe*, *suppose*, and *expect*.
I **don't expect** we'll meet again.
My friends **didn't believe** I'd do a bungee jump!

2 We can also use *seem*, *expect*, and *want* with the negative (+ object) + infinitive:
She **doesn't** seem **to be** very happy.
I **don't** expect **to get** the job.
I **don't** want **to go back** to that restaurant.
He **doesn't** expect **us to pass** the exams.

Rewrite the sentences, using the verb in brackets in the negative.

1 You haven't met my wife. (think)

   I don't think you've met my wife.

2 You haven't got change for a 20-euro note. (suppose)

   I _____ .

3 This machine isn't working. (seem)

   This machine _____ .

4 It wasn't going to rain. (think)

   I _____ .

5 Their daughter's moving to Canada. They aren't happy. (want)

   They _____ .

6 I'm surprised to see you here. (expect)

   I _____ .

7 You haven't seen Robert recently. (suppose)

   I _____ .

8 I wouldn't like snails. (think)

   I _____ .

9 You probably don't remember me. (expect)

   I _____ .

10 She didn't pass all her exams. (believe)

   I _____ .

8 Not the whole truth!

White lies are what we say to people so as not to upset them or to get out of an awkward situation.

1 🎧 Listen and match the conversations with the pictures.

2 Now match the pictures (A–H) to what the people are really thinking.

1 **H** Only 100 mph! Actually, it was 110.

2 ☐ Really? You look 40-plus!

3 ☐ I went for a drink with friends from work.

4 ☐ That dress is too tight for you.

5 ☐ What a boring present!

6 ☐ Oh help! My mouth is on fire!

7 ☐ Great! I managed to get away without paying.

8 ☐ What an ugly baby!

Prepositions

9 Verb + preposition

Many verbs are followed by prepositions. Complete the sentences with the correct preposition.

1 I agree **with** every word you say.
2 I applied _____ the job, but I didn't get it.
3 He died _____ a heart attack.
4 She's suffering _____ a nasty chest infection.
5 Do you believe _____ magic?
6 I didn't realize Maria was married _____ George.
7 Don't you think Mike's been acting _____ a very strange way?
8 Did you succeed _____ convincing your father you were telling the truth?
9 Compared _____ you, I'm not very intelligent at all!
10 We've complained _____ our teacher _____ the amount of homework we get.
11 Stop laughing _____ me. It isn't funny!
12 I've completely fallen _____ love _____ you.
13 Who will you vote _____ in the next election?
14 Bollywood sensation Katrina Kaif has appeared _____ over 30 films.

Vocabulary

10 Antonyms and synonyms

1 For the words in **A**, write their opposites in **B**, using prefixes.

A	B	C
Adjectives		
real	<u>unreal</u>	<u>fake</u>
truthful		
credible		
plausible		
probable		
pleased		
normal		
professional		
important		
Nouns		
honesty		
reality		
belief		
Verbs		
appear		
understand		
trust		
cover		

2 In column **C**, write synonyms for the words in **B**, using the words in the box.

~~fake~~	confuse	dishonest	reveal
deceit	unbelievable	fantasy	vanish
ridiculous	annoyed	bizarre	amateur
unlikely	trivial	incredulity	suspect

Pronunciation

11 Intonation in question tags

🔊 In question tags the intonation either falls ↘ or rises ↗.

1 ↘ Falling intonation means that the sentence is more like a statement = 'I'm sure I'm right. Can you just confirm this for me?'

2 ↗ Rising intonation means that the sentence is more like a real question = 'I'm not sure if I'm right about this. Correct me if I'm wrong.'

You've lost the car keys again, haven't you?

You've been invited to Jane's party, haven't you?

Both patterns are very common in spoken English because they invite other people to join in the conversation.

---

1 🔊 Write the question tags for the statements. Mark whether it falls or rises.

1 It's really warm again today, <u>isn't it</u> ? ↘

2 You're angry with me, _____ ?

3 Last night was such a hot night, _____ ?

4 You couldn't help me carry this bag, _____ ?

5 Antonio's late again, _____ ?

6 It's cold for this time of year, _____ ?

7 John didn't fail his driving test again, _____ ?

8 You haven't seen my pen anywhere, _____ ?

9 By the end of the film we were all in tears, _____ ?

10 You wouldn't have change for a £10 note, _____ ?

2 🔊 Write a sentence and a question tag for these situations and mark the intonation pattern.

1 You ask Tom if he could help you do your homework.

<u>Tom, you couldn't help me with my homework, could you?</u> ↗

2 You're coming out of a restaurant where you have just had a really tasteless meal with a friend.

That _____ ?

3 You can't believe that your sister has borrowed your new coat again.

You _____ ?

4 You need a neighbour to water your plants while you're away.

You _____ ?

5 You think that Vanessa is going on a business trip to Rome next week, but you're not sure.

Vanessa, you _____ ?

Future forms • Conjunctions in time clauses
• Commonly confused words • Phrasal verbs – types 2 and 3
• Sounds and spelling

Looking ahead

Future forms

1 Question tags

Match a sentence in **A** with a question tag in **B**.

A	B
1 You're going to work harder from now on,	8 will we?
2 I'll see you next week,	5 doesn't it?
3 Kate's leaving soon,	9 won't we?
4 You'll ring when you get there,	7 are you?
5 Our plane takes off at 4 p.m.,	2 won't I?
6 The painters will have finished by next week,	3 isn't she?
7 You aren't getting married next week,	4 won't you?
8 We won't need tickets to get in,	6 won't they?
9 We'll be millionaires one day,	10 will he?
10 Max won't be coming,	1 aren't you?

"I just have a feeling that my son
is not going to grow up to be a farmer."

2 *will* or *going to*?

Complete the conversations with *will* or *going to* in the
correct form. Sometimes there is more than one answer.

1 **A** I _am going to_ make myself a sandwich. Do you
want one?

   B No, thanks. I _will_ have something later.

2 **A** Marco and Lia _are going to_ spend their
honeymoon in Venice.

   B How wonderful! I'm sure they _will_ love
it!

3 **A** Bye, Mum. I _am going to_ meet Tom and Mel.
I _will_ be back at about ten o'clock.

   B OK, but don't be late again or I _will_ be
really annoyed.

4 **A** Jo _will_ be furious when she finds out
I've crashed the car.

   B She _will_ understand if you explain that
it wasn't your fault.

5 **A** I've just seen the weather forecast and it
is going to be chilly again.

   B I think I _will_ take a coat then.

6 **A** I'm tired. I think I _will_ go to bed.

   B I _am going to_ watch the news, then I
will join you.

7 **A** My boss has told me I _am going to_ be promoted.

   B Congratulations! We _will_ have to
celebrate!

8 **A** Mr Smith, now you've won the lottery you
will be the fifth-richest man in England.
How do you feel about that?

   B I _will_ tell you next week. I'm too
shocked at the moment!

3 What does John say?

Write what John actually says in these situations. Use a future form.

1 He sees some very black clouds in the sky.

> It's going to rain.

2 His sister has just reminded him that it is his grandmother's birthday soon.

> I _____ _____ _____.

3 He has decided to study hard for his final exams.

> I _____ _____ _____.

4 He's made an appointment to see the dentist next Friday.

> I _____ _____ _____.

5 He predicts a win for his team, Manchester United, on Saturday.

> I think _____ _____ _____.

6 He's stuck in a traffic jam. He's late for a meeting. He rings his office.

> I'm sorry. _____ _____ _____.

7 His sister is pregnant. The baby is due next March.

> My sister _____ _____ _____.

8 His plane ticket for next Sunday says: Departure 7.30 a.m. London, Heathrow.

> My plane _____ _____ _____.

9 He can see himself lying on a beach in Spain next week at this time.

> This time next week _____ _____.

10 He predicts hot weather there.

> I think it _____ _____ _____.

4 Future Continuous or Future Perfect?
By the time I'm 30 …

1 🎧 Listen to Tommy (**T**), Jack (**J**), and Millie (**M**) talking about their futures. Who wants to …

become a pilot? __T__

work in the US?

live in the north of England?

move to London?

travel the world?

study law?

buy a farm?

win an Olympic medal?

mix with celebrities?

design swimwear?

marry a film star?

live near the river?

buy a penthouse flat?

go clubbing and partying?

2 🎧 Listen again and complete the sentences about what Tommy, Jack, and Millie will have done or will be doing by the time they are 30.

By the time Tommy is 30, …

1 _he'll be flying for British Airways._

2 _he will have moved to London._

3 _____

4 _____

5 _____

By the time Jack is 30, …

1 _he_ _____

2 _____

3 _____

4 _____

By the time Millie is 30, …

1 _she_ _____

2 _____

3 _____

4 _____

5 An inspirational teenager

Read the interview and (circle) the best future form.

Dreams Can Come True

Meet Noah Grey, a young gymnast with high aspirations for the next Olympics.

I Hello, Noah. It is good of you to be interviewed today, as I know you have a busy training schedule.

N That's OK. I ¹ *'ll take / 'm taking* a couple of days off anyway as it's my birthday tomorrow. I ² *'m / 'm going to be* 18 – an adult at last.

I Only 18 and you've accomplished so much already! You won a bronze medal at the European Championships last year, and I know you ³ *'ll be hoping / 'll have hoped* to win gold at the next Olympics.

N That's my dream. I ⁴ *'ll never give up / 'll never be giving up* until I've done all I can to achieve it. That's what keeps me going through the hours of training. I keep telling myself it'll be worth it if I ⁵ *win / will win* gold. Failure isn't an option.

I You're very tough on yourself, Noah. That's a lot of commitment and hard work. You're still young. Surely you must spend time with friends.

N No, gymnastics is everything to me. I ⁶ *'ll be training / 'll have been training* intensively for six years by the next Olympics, and every minute of practice will help.

I The World Championships ⁷ *are being staged / are staged* in China next year. How are you preparing for this competition?

N Well, I'm good at the pommel horse and the parallel bars, so by the time the Championships start, I ⁸ *concentrate / 'll have concentrated* on them most. I think the bars ⁹ *will be / are being* my best event.

I Will you ¹⁰ *be hoping / have hoped* for a medal?

N Yes, I ¹¹ *will / have*. Maybe silver or bronze.

I You're such a role model for young people today. Do you have any advice for other young hopefuls?

N Yes, never lose sight of your dream. If you work hard, you ¹² *will have been / will be* successful.

I Thank you, Noah. I wish you all the best and Happy Birthday for tomorrow.

Conjunctions in time clauses

6 Future time clauses

1 Notice that in clauses after *if, when, as soon as, until, before, after, once,* and *unless,* we normally use a present tense to talk about the future. A future form is not used.

> *I'll phone you* **when I arrive**. NOT *when I'll arrive*
> *I won't marry you* **unless you give up** *smoking!*
> NOT *unless you'll give up*

2 To show that the first action will be completed before the second, we use the Present Perfect..

> *I'll fax you the report* **as soon as I've written it**.
> *They're going to emigrate to Australia* **after the baby has been born**.

Complete the sentences with the verbs in brackets in the correct tense.

1 Unless you _____ (eat) something, you _____ (not get) better.

2 We _____ (not move) to Paris until we _____ (find) a flat there to rent.

3 You _____ (love) Adam when you _____ (meet) him. He's so funny.

4 _____ you _____ (learn) to drive as soon as you _____ (be) 17?

5 The children _____ (not go) to bed unless they _____ (have) a glass of milk.

6 It _____ (be) at least an hour before I _____ (finish) this report.

7 If you _____ (not do) well in the test, _____ you _____ (have to) do it again?

8 As soon as we _____ (be) able to process the information, we _____ (deal) with your request.

9 The doctor says that I _____ (feel) much better once I _____ (have) the operation.

10 Once you _____ (try) 'Glowhite' toothpaste, you _____ (never use) anything else!

7 Check it

In these conversations, some of the future forms are wrong. Find the mistakes and correct them.

1 ☑ **A** Have you heard? Sue's going to have a baby.
   ☐ **B** Really? ~~I'm going to~~ *I'll* give her a ring
      this evening to congratulate her.

2 ☐ **A** What do you do this weekend?
   ☐ **B** I don't know yet. Maybe I'll give
      Paul a ring and see what he's doing.

3 ☐ **A** I'll be honest with you, Matthew. I don't
      think you're going to pass this exam.
   ☐ **B** Oh, no! What will I be doing?

4 ☐ **A** Is it true that Rachel will go to the
      States to work as a nanny?
   ☐ **B** Yes, and guess what! I am, too!

5 ☐ **A** Our plane leaves at six o'clock on Saturday
      morning.
   ☐ **B** You have to wake me up. I can never get
      up in the mornings.

6 ☐ **A** It's my birthday tomorrow. I'm going to be 30!
   ☐ **B** 30! That's ancient! You are getting your
      pension soon.

7 ☐ **A** My parents will be arriving soon, and the
      house looks like a pigsty.
   ☐ **B** Don't worry. It'll only be taking a few minutes
      to clear up.

8 ☐ **A** Will you be going skiing as usual after
      Christmas?
   ☐ **B** Not this year. It's just too expensive. We'll stay
      at home.

9 ☐ **A** I'll ring you as soon as I'll arrive.
   ☐ **B** Please do. We'll be waiting to hear you've
      arrived safely.

10 ☐ **A** Are you going to Sam's party on Friday?
   ☐ **B** Yeah, unless I am getting held up at work.

Vocabulary

8 Hot verbs – *take, put*

Complete the conversation between Kerry and Daisy
with the correct form of *take* or *put*.

K Hi, Kerry. Are you thinking of [1] _____ part in
that acting competition? Second prize is tickets for
Emma Watson's new film. You're a big fan of hers,
aren't you?

D She's my heroine. I think she's just brilliant. If she
[2] _____ her mind to it, she can do anything.

K Aren't you [3] _____ her on a pedestal? She was
OK in the Harry Potter films, but she's not that great.

D What! She's done so much more than Harry Potter.
She [4] _____ up modelling and won a People's
Choice award for her latest film.

K Pretty impressive stuff, I suppose. Isn't she studying
as well?

D She certainly is. She [5] _____ some time off
university to promote her films, but she's back there
now and finishing her degree.

K OK, sorry – I ⁶_____ back what I said. It's not fair, is it? Some people have all the luck.

D Come on! You've been offered a good part in *Shrek the Musical*. I think your acting career is about to ⁷_____ off!

K It's not a very big part. I'm just in the chorus.

D Don't ⁸_____ yourself down. If you ⁹_____ in enough effort, you'll become a star. You've got a great singing voice, too.

K Oh Daisy, do you really think so?

D Yeah, I do. Our music coach has really ¹⁰_____ to you. She thinks you've got real promise. You'll be famous one day.

K We both will! Come on! Let's ¹¹_____ our names down for this competition.

D And if one of us wins, they'll have to ¹²_____ the other out for a meal.

K Deal!

🎧 Listen and check.

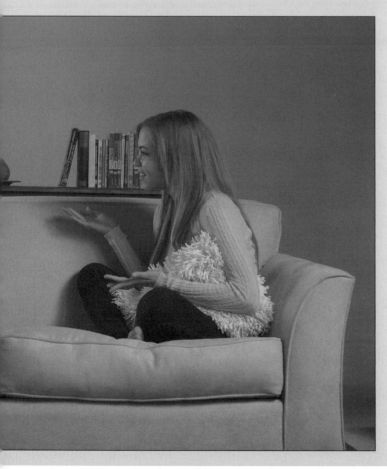

9 Commonly confused words

Complete the sentences using the words in the box in the correct form.

| expect | wait for | look forward to |

1 a We _____ the rain to stop so that we can play tennis.

   b The weather forecast says a lot of rain _____ over the next few days.

   c I'm very excited. I'm _____ starting my new job at the bank.

| pass | spend | waste |

2 a I _____ too much time with my mates and not enough time with my girlfriend.

   b I usually read the newspaper to _____ the time on train journeys.

   c I _____ my time at school. I wish I'd tried harder and studied more.

| see | watch | look at |

3 a _____ you _____ that new Spielberg film yet?

   b The police sat in their car. They _____ every move the men made.

   c _____ this picture little Amy has painted!

| actually | at the moment | really |

4 a **A** What a shame James lost the match!

      B _____ , he won.

   b The kids are playing in the garden _____ .

   c Love that dress. You _____ look wonderful!

| lend | borrow | owe |

5 a I have a student loan. I _____ the bank £10,000, which is a big debt.

   b Jed _____ £5,000 from the bank to buy a car.

   c Could you _____ me £20 until the end of the week? I'm broke.

| angry | nervous | embarrassed |

6 a He felt _____ when he realized that he couldn't remember her name.

   b I'm very _____ about my interview tomorrow.

   c We're _____ with the government for not listening to us.

Phrasal verbs

10 Type 2 and type 3

Type 2 and type 3 phrasal verbs have an object and a particle.

Type 2

The particle can move position. NOTE A particle always comes after pronouns (*him, it, me,* etc.).

> ***Take off*** *your coat.* ***Take*** *your coat* ***off***.
> ***Take*** *it* ***off***. NOT ~~Take off it~~.
> *I* ***put on*** *the DVD. I* ***put*** *the DVD* ***on***.
> *I* ***put*** *it* ***on***. NOT ~~I put on it~~.

Type 3

The particle cannot move.

> ***Look after*** *your sister.*
> NOT ~~Look your sister after~~.
> ~~Look her after~~.
>
> *I'll* ***look into*** *the problem.*
> NOT ~~I'll look the problem into~~.
> ~~I'll look it into~~.

Dictionaries indicate the type of phrasal verb by the position of the particle in the dictionary entry.

put sth on The particle is shown *after* **sth**. (Type 2)

look into sth The particle is shown *before* **sth**. (Type 3)

Put a pronoun in the correct place in these sentences.

1 Listen to this song. I'll put **it** on **–** for you.

2 I know you've got a lot of problems, but I'm sure you'll get **–** through **them** .

3 I can't remember the directions. I couldn't take _____ all in _____ .

4 There's a problem with my computer. I'll sort _____ out _____ tomorrow.

5 We're having a meeting on the 25th. Put _____ in _____ your diary.

6 There are clothes all over your bedroom. Please put _____ away _____ .

7 If you're going out with your little brother, you'd better look _____ after _____ .

8 I'm sorry you had a complaint about your room. I'll look _____ into _____ right away.

9 That was a mean thing you said! Take _____ back _____ !

10 I liked Ann, but since you told me what she did, you've put me _____ off _____ .

Pronunciation

11 Sounds and spelling

1 🎧 Listen and match the letters <u>underlined</u> in each word with the correct sound.

1 w<u>o</u>n't	/ʌ/	/əʊ/	/ɒ/
2 w<u>a</u>lk	/ɔː/	/ɑː/	/ɒ/
3 w<u>o</u>nder	/ʌ/	/ɔː/	/ɒ/
4 w<u>o</u>man	/ʊ/	/əʊ/	/ʌ/
5 w<u>a</u>rm	/ɔː/	/aɪ/	/ɜː/
6 w<u>o</u>rd	/ɔː/	/ɜː/	/aɪ/
7 w<u>ea</u>r	/eə/	/e/	/iː/
8 w<u>ei</u>ght	/aɪ/	/eɪ/	/e/
9 w<u>a</u>nt	/æ/	/əʊ/	/ɒ/
10 w<u>o</u>rk	/ɔː/	/ɜː/	/ɔɪ/
11 w<u>a</u>nder	/ʌ/	/ɔː/	/ɒ/
12 w<u>o</u>men	/ʊ/	/əʊ/	/ɪ/
13 w<u>o</u>rm	/ɔː/	/ɔɪ/	/ɜː/
14 w<u>a</u>rd	/ɑː/	/aɪ/	/ɔː/
15 w<u>ea</u>ry	/eə/	/ɪə/	/iː/
16 w<u>ei</u>rd	/aɪ/	/eɪ/	/ɪə/

2 🎧 In each group of words, three words rhyme. (Circle) the odd one out.

1	/ʌ/	done	phone	won	son
2	/ʊ/	would	should	good	blood
3	/uː/	move	love	prove	groove
4	/əʊ/	though	through	throw	sew
5	/eɪ/	weak	break	ache	shake
6	/aʊ/	flower	power	tower	lower
7	/ɜː/	worth	birth	north	earth
8	/eɪ/	hate	wait	weight	height
9	/ɪə/	fear	near	pear	clear
10	/eə/	share	bear	fair	hear

6

Countable and uncountable nouns • Expressing quantity
• Compounds with *some, any, no, every* • Money
• Prepositions • Words with variable stress

Hitting the big time

Countable and uncountable nouns

1 Countable or uncountable?

(Circle) the noun in each group that is uncountable.

1 cheque coin cash salary bonus

2 job employee boss unemployment profession

3 motorway traffic traffic jam hold-up rush hour

4 holiday journey flight luggage suitcase

5 meal dish food menu dessert

6 pop group musical music opera concert

7 arrest violence accident crime criminal

(Circle) the noun in each group that is usually countable.

8 luck happiness opportunity fun help

9 ingredient cutlery fruit meat food

10 fresh air sleep fluid health energy

2 *some* or *any*?

Complete the sentences with *some* or *any*.

1 Why don't you ask your father to lend you _____ money? I haven't got _____ .

2 _____ people don't have _____ problems learning foreign languages.

3 Would you like _____ more fizzy mineral water?
I don't want _____ more.

4 My teenage sister never has _____ difficulty learning the words of the latest pop songs. There are hardly _____ she doesn't know by heart.

5 I didn't realize that there was still _____ coffee left. I've made _____ more.

6 I did this exercise without _____ help.

3 *much* or *many*?

Rewrite the sentences using the words in brackets and *much* or *many*. Make any other necessary changes.

1 I'm not sure how much drink to buy. (cans of cola)

   <u>I'm not sure how many cans of cola to buy.</u>

2 Are there many jobs to be done in the garden? (work)

   _____

3 I didn't spend many hours on the homework. (time)

   _____

4 Did they do many experiments before they found a cure? (research)

   _____

5 I didn't have too much difficulty with this exercise either. (problems)

   _____

6 I've got too many suitcases. I can't carry them all. (luggage)

   _____

7 There are too many cars and lorries on the streets of our town. (traffic)

   _____

8 They couldn't give me many details about the delay to our flight. (information)

   _____

4 The canteen

1 Look at the picture of the students' canteen. Write ten sentences, using each expression in the box once.

several	a couple of	a few	not much	lots of
not many	a little	hardly any	no	a huge amount of

1 _____

2 _____

3 _____

4 _____

5 _____

6 _____

7 _____

8 _____

9 _____

10 _____

2 🎧 Answer the students' questions, using an expression of quantity without a noun.

1 Is there any chocolate cake?
Sorry, there's **none** left.

2 What about rice?
Well, there's **a little** .

3 Can I have some spaghetti?
Yes, of course, there's _____ left.

4 Have you got lots of tuna sandwiches?
Well, there are _____ .

5 Two vegetable curries, please.
Sorry, there's _____ left.

6 Can I have some chips with my burger?
Sorry, there are _____ left.

7 Have you got apple pie today?
Yes, just _____ .

8 Are there any chocolate biscuits?
Well, there are _____ .

9 Can I have a large portion of fruit salad, please?
Sorry, there's only _____ left.

10 Have you run out of bananas?
No, I think we've got _____ out the back.

11 **A** Is this all the apple juice you've got?

 B Yes, I'm afraid there are only _____ cartons left.

 A OK, I'll take those, and three of orange juice, please.

 B No problem, we've got _____ of orange.

5 *very little, a little, very few, a few, fewer, less*

Rewrite the sentences with *very little, a little, very few, a few, fewer,* or *less*. Change all the <u>underlined</u> words.

1 There was a lot of wine at the party, but <u>hardly any</u> was drunk. **very little**

2 I'm on a diet so I'll just have <u>three</u> crackers and <u>a small piece of</u> cheese.

3 Children <u>don't</u> have <u>as much</u> respect <u>as</u> they used to for their teachers.

4 Lots of people have tried to climb Everest, but <u>not many</u> have succeeded.

5 Dave can speak fluent Norwegian and <u>some</u> Swedish.

6 <u>Not as many</u> people smoke these days.

7 <u>Not many</u> people manage to become completely fluent in a language.

8 It's been <u>three or four</u> years since we last saw him.

9 There <u>isn't</u> very <u>much</u> I can do to help you.

10 There are lots of reasons why I don't want to expand the business. Here are <u>some</u> of them.

Compounds with *some, any, no, every*

6 *something, anybody, nowhere, everyone ...*

1 *Any, anyone, anybody, anywhere,* and *anything* can mean it doesn't matter which/who/where/what.

Put the picture **anywhere**, I don't mind.
You can say **anything** you want. I don't care.
Borrow **any** book you want.

2 *Everybody* and *everything* are singular, not plural.
   Everybody knows who did it.

Everyone likes John.

---

1 Complete the sentences with a combination of these words.

some / any / no / every **+** one / body / thing / where

1 I don't care where we go on holiday as long as it's _____ hot.

2 Does _____ want a cup of tea?

3 I've looked for my contact lens, but I can't find it _____ .

4 **A** What do you want for dinner, Harry?

   B Oh, _____ , I don't mind!

5 This sale is fantastic. There's 50% off _____ in the shop.

6 It's really boring at Auntie Martha's, there's absolutely _____ to do.

7 I'm a very sensitive person. _____ understands me.

8 There was _____ for me to sit on the train so I had to stand.

9 Jane's getting engaged to _____ she met on holiday.

10 Sue is such a chatterbox; she's always got _____ to say, but she never says _____ interesting.

11 Our dog will go for a walk with _____ .

12 Tommy's so popular. _____ likes him.

2 Match a line in **A** with a line in **B** to make sentences.

A		B	
1	He told them he knew	a	anything.
2	He didn't tell them	b	nothing.
3	I think they live	c	somewhere near here.
4	I don't mind. I'll live	d	anywhere near here.
5	Anybody	e	phoned you. Sorry!
6	Nobody	f	can cook. It's easy.
7	I've searched	g	anywhere.
8	I can't find it	h	everywhere.
9	I thought I'd know	i	somebody at the party.
10	I didn't know	j	anyone at the party.
11	My parents never took me	k	everywhere.
12	My parents took me	l	anywhere.
13	Jane always got	m	everything she wanted.
14	Jane didn't have	n	anything to wear.
15	I've already had	o	something to eat.
16	I've had	p	nothing to eat.

Expressing quantity

7 If at first you don't succeed

Read about three entrepreneurs. Complete their stories using the words in the boxes.

If at first you don't succeed ...

In reality TV programme *Dragons' Den*, hopeful entrepreneurs pitch their business ideas to a panel of multi-millionaires. The 'Dragons' invest if they believe the business is viable. But sometimes they are wrong ...

The Trunki

any	a bit	all	few
many	one piece	one of	

The Trunki is a colourful, adaptable piece of hand luggage for children which
[1] _____ of us will have seen at airports. It is a small suitcase with wheels, which can be used as a seat for children who are getting [2] _____ tired, or easily pulled by a parent with a small child sitting on top. The Trunki is a great invention and
[3] _____ parents travelling by plane with young children would disagree.
Despite its obvious potential, the inventor of the Trunki, Rob Law, was dismissed from the Den without [4] _____ financial backing.
The Trunki is now [5] _____ the top-selling baggage items at department stores in the UK.
Rob offers [6] _____ new entrepreneurs
[7] _____ of advice:
'If at first you don't succeed, try, try, try again.'

The SwimFin

hundred	a couple	all
anything	more	
something	nobody	

Kevin Moseley is an inventor with a sense of humour. He came up with the idea of designing a shark's fin to help children float in water! His invention was rejected by [8] _____ of the Dragons, who even made [9] _____ of *Jaws* jokes. They said [10] _____ would buy such a 'dangerous' and 'silly' swimming aid and that his SwimFin would never amount to
[11] _____.
However, Kevin decided to ignore their comments and make
[12] _____ SwimFins in his garage. Two years later, the SwimFin is a [13] _____-thousand pound business and a worldwide success,
[14] _____ the Dragons hadn't anticipated!

Destination London

any	a great deal	none	several
everything	no one	more than	

[15] _____ is a better example of never giving up than Rachel Lowe. She took her Destination London board game to the Den where she was subjected to [16] _____ of ridicule from the Dragons. [17] _____ of them saw a future in the game, and she left without [18] _____ investment.
However, Rachel had the last laugh when [19] _____ months later Destination London sold [20] _____ any other toy at the world-famous toy store, Hamleys. The Destination brand now comprises over 20 editions, including a Harry Potter version.
Unfortunately, because of the banking crises, Rachel's company went into administration, and she lost [21] _____ . Rachel never gave up, though, and launched a new fragrance and accessories brand, 'She Who Dares'.

Vocabulary

8 Money advice

1 Read the advice on how to manage your money. Complete 1–8 with verbs from the box.

Moneymatters

About us
FAQs
News
Forums

At Moneymatters we are committed to getting you the best [1] *deals* in all your money matters. We always encourage you, the [2] *consumer*, to negotiate with companies to get [3] *rock-bottom* prices.

For 0% interest balance transfers, [4] *contrast* credit cards deals. Always read the small print – they might offer 0% interest, but there could be a [5] *large* transfer fee.

Thousands of people pay too much for services provided by their bank. If your bank's [6] *fees* look very high, they may be [7] *unlawful*. Check your bank's fees with those of other banks, and if you can show unfair differences between them, you may be able to get a refund.

[8] *Arrange* direct debits rather than write cheques. This will mean that money [9] *goes out of* your account on a specific date every month – you won't make payments late, and you won't be charged fees or interest.

Be careful when buying foreign currency. £100 can buy at best 124 euros and at worst 113! Find the best exchange rates online. You could be literally throwing your money away if you don't.

URGENT! [10] *Cut* your household costs by fixing your gas and electricity bills now. There's going to be a large [11] *increase in* energy prices this year, and an agreed price between you and your supplier could make a considerable difference to your household [12] *expenditure*.

set up   reduce   spread   reclaim   haggle   transfer   compare   pay off

1 You can _____ your heating bill by up to 20% by insulating your loft.

2 You should _____ your credit card balance to a new card with 0% interest.

3 You can _____ unfair bank charges by contacting your bank directly.

4 Before renewing your car insurance, go online and _____ prices. You could be paying far too much!

5 You should always _____ over your mobile phone package, you can usually negotiate a better deal!

6 Rather than paying in full, _____ the cost of household bills over the year in monthly or quarterly payments.

7 To manage your finances more efficiently, _____ direct debits, then you know exactly when money is leaving your bank account.

8 It is always advisable to _____ credit card balances in full each month to avoid paying high interest charges.

2 Read the text again. Which words from the box can replace the words in *italics*?

customer ☐	hefty ☐	hike ☐	charges ☐	set up ☐	leaves ☐
bargains ☐	slash ☐	the lowest ☐	compare ☐	illegal ☐	outgoings ☐

Prepositions

9 Prepositions and nouns that go together

Which prepositions go with the words on the right in these two tables?

A						
below	in	on	over	under	against	
✓		✓				average
						debt
						arrest
						Arabic
						75%
						freezing
						18 years old
						the advice
						new management
						holiday
						pressure
						business

B						
at	by	during	in	on	from	
✓	✓					midnight
						the night
						the beginning
						New Year's Day
						the winter
						Friday afternoon
						the weekend
						time
						a fortnight's time
						the rush hour
						his forties
						the end of the week

10 Prepositions in context

Complete the article with prepositions.

The Story of LEGO

The world-famous LEGO company has its origins in the workshop of a poor Danish carpenter, Ole Kirk Christiansen [1] _____ the first half of the 20th century. [2] _____ these humble beginnings, it has grown to become one of the most popular toys [3] _____ all time.

Ole, the tenth son in the family, earned a living making toys with his father. Finally, he became a master carpenter and [4] _____ 1932 he set up his own business making toys and wooden bricks. He called the company LEGO, which means 'play well' [5] _____ Danish. Unfortunately, ten years later his factory burned down. However, despite being [6] _____ great financial pressure, Ole had it rebuilt. This took three years and [7] _____ that time he learnt of a British company which specialized [8] _____ plastic moulding machines. His managers thought they were too expensive, but [9] _____ their advice, Ole bought one. It was worth the investment. [10] _____ the end of the decade, the company was producing a successful range of toys and interlocking bricks, and Ole's son, Godtfred, had joined him [11] _____ the business.

Sadly, Ole didn't live to see the success of his company. He died [12] _____ the age of 66 and Godtfred became Managing Director. The modern brick design was patented [13] _____ 28 January 1958, and bricks from that year are still compatible [14] _____ bricks today.

Unbelievably, [15] _____ the 1960s, the LEGO factory was struck [16] _____ lightening and burned [17] _____ the ground again. After this, Godtfred had to rethink the direction of the company. This time, [18] _____ the advice of his directors, he decided to concentrate solely [19] _____ the hugely successful interlocking plastic bricks.

Godtfred's son, Kjeld, is the current Deputy-Chairman and to celebrate the company's 80th anniversary, a short animated film called 'The LEGO story' was released [20] _____ August 2012.

Facts and figures

1 Today, the LEGO club has 4.7 million members worldwide.
2 On average, every person on Earth owns 86 LEGO bricks.
3 A column of 40 billion LEGO bricks would reach the moon.
4 Ten LEGO sets are sold every second.
5 The number of bricks sold yearly would go 18 times round the world.

Ole, Godtfred, and Kjeld Christiansen, three generations of LEGO men.

Listening

11 A job interview

1 🎧 Listen to the interview. Which job is Jane going for?

WANTED

A motivated and enthusiastic sales person to sell Commodore cosmetics at our beauty department at Selfridges, London. Minimum two years' experience in cosmetic sales.

RECEPTIONIST

A business-focused receptionist needed for a busy law office in central Bristol. Experience desirable. Immediate start required.

SALES REPRESENTATIVE

Full-time sales representative needed for South West region. A proven track-record in sales essential. Knowledge of UK pet market desirable.

2 🎧 Listen again and complete the sentences.

1 No, I live near Bristol so it was _____ 30 minutes …

2 Do you know _____ about our company?

3 … and you are _____ pet food companies …

4 … and is a market bestseller endorsed by _____ high-profile celebrity pet owners.

5 You seem to know _____ about our company.

6 Could you give me _____ information on your key skills …

7 … I was always able to work on my own _____ guidance.

8 I used to feel anxious about giving presentations to _____ people …

9 … been on _____ courses which have made a huge difference.

Pronunciation

12 Words with variable stress

1 🎧 Listen to the pronunciation of the words. Write **N** for noun and **V** for verb.

1 ☐ refuse	7 ☐ permit
2 ☐ transport	8 ☐ record
3 ☐ produce	9 ☐ contract
4 ☐ decrease	10 ☐ desert
5 ☐ progress	11 ☐ present
6 ☐ insult	12 ☐ content

2 Read this news item aloud. Pay attention to the shifting stress on words that are both verbs and nouns.

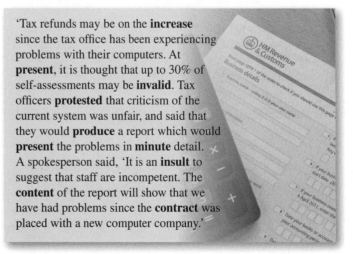

'Good evening. Here is the news. Oil imports continued to increase in the last quarter. The cost of transport fuel is already at record levels, and the Prime Minister refuses to rule out further increases. Members of the Transport Workers' Union insist that they will protest against any future price rises. They presented a report maintaining that present fuel price increases are due to a decrease in investment in railway transport by the government.'

🎧 Listen and check. Practise reading the text again.

3 Read this news item and mark the stress on the words in **bold**. Then read it aloud, paying attention to the shifting stress.

'Tax refunds may be on the **increase** since the tax office has been experiencing problems with their computers. At **present**, it is thought that up to 30% of self-assessments may be **invalid**. Tax officers **protested** that criticism of the current system was unfair, and said that they would **produce** a report which would **present** the problems in **minute** detail. A spokesperson said, 'It is an **insult** to suggest that staff are incompetent. The **content** of the report will show that we have had problems since the **contract** was placed with a new computer company.'

🎧 Listen and check. Practise reading the texts again.

7

Modal auxiliary verbs • *need* • Verbs related to modals
• Phrasal verbs – type 4 • Consonant clusters • Sentence stress

Getting along

Revision of all modals

1 Meaning check

Tick (✓) the correct explanation for each of these modals.

1 Leanne may look for a new job.
   a ☐ Leanne has permission to look for a new job.
   b ☐ It's possible Leanne will look for a new job.

2 I couldn't swim until I was 16.
   a ☐ I wasn't allowed to swim until I was 16.
   b ☐ I wasn't able to swim until I was 16.

3 No one can smoke in pubs or restaurants.
   a ☐ No one is allowed to smoke in pubs or restaurants.
   b ☐ No one is able to smoke in pubs or restaurants.

4 You should wear glasses.
   a ☐ My advice is that you wear glasses.
   b ☐ It's possible that you will have to wear glasses.

5 Will you answer the phone?
   a ☐ I'm asking you to answer the phone.
   b ☐ Are you at some time in the future going to answer the phone?

6 I couldn't get the top off the jar.
   a ☐ I didn't manage to get the top off the jar.
   b ☐ I wasn't allowed to get the top off the jar.

7 You must be tired.
   a ☐ You are required to be tired.
   b ☐ I'm sure you are tired.

8 Andy's very busy, so he may not go to the party.
   a ☐ Andy doesn't have permission to go to the party.
   b ☐ There's a possibility Andy won't go to the party.

2 Which modal?

1 Complete the sentences with words from the box. Often there is more than one answer.

will	should	can	ought to	could
must	may	have to	might	

1 You _____ get your hair cut. It's too long.

2 _____ I ask you a question?

3 Young children _____ be carried on this escalator.

4 You _____ never get a seat on this train. It's always packed.

5 I _____ be studying Mandarin Chinese next year.

6 I _____ already speak five languages fluently.

7 You'll _____ work much harder if you want to pass.

8 It's Saturday night. There _____ be something good on TV.

9 You _____ leave your valuables in the hotel safe.

10 You _____ be over 1m 60cm tall to be a flight attendant.

2 (Circle) the correct answer.

1 You *mustn't / won't* have any problems with Josh. He's such a good baby.

2 You *don't have to / mustn't* use cream in this sauce, but it makes it much tastier.

3 I *couldn't / wouldn't* watch my favourite programme because Mia rang up for a long chat.

4 Timmy's so stubborn. He just *can't / won't* do what he's told.

5 I'm afraid I *can't / may not* come to your wedding as I'll be in Australia.

6 I *was able to / could* get 20% off the price in the sale.

7 You *don't have to / mustn't* say a word about this to your mother. It's a surprise.

3 Positive to negative

Rewrite the sentences to make them negative.

1 You must stop here.

_____

2 We must learn the whole poem.

_____

3 They had to take off their shoes.

_____

4 He must be speaking Swedish.

_____

5 They will have to wear a uniform at their new school.

_____

6 You'll have to help me do this exercise.

_____

4 Present probability

Respond to the statements or questions using the words in brackets. Put the verb in its correct form.

1 Harry is packing his suitcase. (must /go on holiday)

  He must be going on holiday.

2 Jenny looks really unhappy. (must / miss / boyfriend)

_____

3 Who's at the front door? (will / Tom)

_____

4 Where's Kate? It's nearly lunchtime! (can't / still / sleep)

_____

5 Why are all the lights on in their house? (could / have / party)

_____

6 James has been working all night. (must / deadline to meet)

_____

7 There's a thick fog this morning. (might / difficult / drive / work)

_____

8 Timmy can't find his little sister. (may / hide / in the garden)

_____

5 need

> Need can work like a modal verb or a normal verb.
> 1 It is usually formed like a normal verb + infinitive with *to*.
>   *She **needs to go** to bed.*
>   *Does she **need to go** to bed?*
>   *She doesn't **need to go** to bed.*
> 2 *Need* is used as a modal verb mainly in the negative.
>   *She **needn't go** to bed yet.*
>   But it can sometimes be used as a question.
>   ***Need I go** to bed?*
> 3 *Need + -ing = need + passive infinitive.*
>   *The car **needs fixing**. = The car needs to be fixed.*

1 Write **M** when *need* is used as a modal verb, and **F** when *need* is used as a full verb.

1 ☐ I need to go home.

2 ☐ You needn't come if you don't want to.

3 ☐ The business doesn't need to invest in more new technology.

4 ☐ Money is desperately needed to protect the world's endangered species.

5 ☐ Need I pay now, or can I pay later?

6 ☐ If you have any problems, you only need to tell us and we'll try to help.

7 ☐ The cooker needs cleaning.

8 ☐ Leave the washing-up. You needn't do it now.

2 (Circle) the correct verb. Sometimes two are correct.

1 I *mustn't / needn't / don't have to* do this exercise but it might help.

2 You *mustn't / needn't / don't have to* think I'm always this irritable. I've just had a bad day.

3 We *mustn't / needn't / don't have to* book a table. The restaurant won't be busy tonight.

4 Do you really *must / need to / have to* go now? Can't you stay a bit longer?

5 You *mustn't / don't need to / don't have to* eat all your vegetables. Just have the carrots.

6 Have I *must / need to / got to* ring and confirm my room reservation?

7 The carpet *needs / must / has to* replacing. Look at the state of it!

6 Modals review

Complete the conversations with a suitable modal verb and the correct form of the verbs in brackets.

1 **A** You really (1) _____ (go) to bed now, or you (2) _____ (feel) tired tomorrow.

   B I'll go in a minute. I (3) _____ (finish) this revision first.

   A You (4) _____ (pass) the exam easily. Get some rest now.

2 **A** It's five past eleven. Ken and Cathy's plane (5) _____ (touch down) in Kennedy Airport right now.

   B Your watch (6) _____ (be) slow. It's nearly half past.

   A It (7) _____ (be)! I've just had it repaired.

3 **A** Bring very warm clothes. It (8) _____ (snow) when we arrive.

   B Oh, yes. I've heard it (9) _____ (snow) in the mountains even in summer.

4 **A** What are all those people doing with those lights and cameras?

   B They (10) _____ (make) a film.

   A Who's the leading man?

   B Not sure. It (11) _____ (be) him over there. And do you think that she's the leading lady?

   A She (12) _____ (be). She's certainly beautiful enough!

5 **A** What are you up to?

   B Just doing the maths homework.

   A Why are you doing that now? We (13) _____ (hand) it in for another week.

   B Well, I (14) _____ (go) away at the weekend, so I want to get it out of the way now.

Vocabulary

7 Verbs related to modals

1 Read the problems and responses. Replace the words in *italics* with a modal verb, or an expression with a modal verb.

Ask Andrea YOUR PROBLEMS SOLVED ONLINE

Drowning in tech!

Dear Andrea,

I think there's something wrong with me. I know technology ¹ *has the potential to* make life easier, but in my case it just makes me terribly anxious as I always feel there are so many things I ² *need to* do. When someone texts, emails, or tweets me, I always think I ³ *need to* reply immediately, and I find it impossible to get anything done! I want to regain some control over my life, but at the moment, I ⁴ *don't* see a way out. I feel like I'm drowning in technology! Please help!

Joanna, Brighton

Joanna, there is nothing wrong with you. This is a problem we all face. Firstly, ⁵ *it is imperative that you* learn how to skim read effectively, then you ⁶ *will be able to* sift quickly through what is important and what isn't. In today's world, this is a skill we ⁷ *need to* develop, otherwise we ⁸ *are certain to* drown, and it's only going to get worse. Also, ⁹ *it is advisable to* prioritize your messages and remember there is no real need to respond immediately. Do you expect an immediate response when you text? I think not, and most of us don't.

Andrea

I must quit!

Dear Andrea,

¹⁰ *It is essential that I* give up smoking. I ¹¹ *am always able to* give up for a few days, but then something stressful happens, and I find myself reaching for the cigarettes. I've noticed that I ¹² *am not able to* run for the bus without gasping for breath, and my girlfriend ¹³ *refuses to* kiss me if I've just been smoking. Please help, I'll try anything.

Graham, Manchester

Graham, you have real motivation to stop, which means you're halfway there. You've already managed without a cigarette for a few days, which shows that ¹⁴ *it is possible for you to* succeed. Recognize that you ¹⁵ *are going to* find it difficult, but that you ¹⁶ *don't* give in to temptation.

There are lots of therapies on the market that ¹⁷ *have the potential to* support you. The highest dosage nicotine patches have the lowest risk of relapse, but lozenges, gum, nasal spray, and inhalers are also available.

¹⁸ *It is advisable that you* start on the higher dose and gradually reduce it to the lower levels. Avoid situations which you associate with smoking. You ¹⁹ *have the ability to* do this. Good luck!

Andrea

2 Rewrite the sentences using the prompts.

1 It's Anna's birthday tomorrow, so I should buy her a card. ('d better)

   It's Anna's birthday tomorrow, so I'd better buy her a card.

2 Guests shouldn't leave valuables in their rooms. (advised)

   _____

3 You can't use your phone in the quiet carriage. (Using … permitted)

   _____

4 I'm sure he'll do well. He's so clever. (bound)

   _____

5 People under 18 shouldn't drink alcohol. (supposed)

   _____

6 You can't use dictionaries in this exam. (The use of dictionaries … allowed)

   _____

7 Travellers to the States need a visa. (required)

   _____

8 I expect you'll find it difficult to learn Russian. (likely)

   _____

9 I wasn't allowed to stay out late until I was 18. (parents … let)

   _____

Phrasal verbs

8 Type 4 – verb + adverb + preposition + object

1. Type 4 phrasal verbs have a verb + adverb + preposition.
The preposition has an object.
*We've **run out of** sugar.*

*Do you **get on with** your neighbours?*

2. The word order cannot change.
*Do you **get on with** them?*
NOT ~~Do you get on them with?~~
*We've **run out of** it.*
NOT ~~We've run out it of.~~

3. Dictionaries show type 4 phrasal verbs by giving both the adverb and the preposition.
get away with sth: do something bad and not get punished for it

4. Sometimes a phrasal verb can be type 4 or type 1.
Type 1: *Their marriage **broke up** last year.*
Type 4: *She's sad because she's just **broken up with** her boyfriend.*
Dictionaries show this.
break up (with sb)

▶▶ Type 1 see p22

Complete the sentences with the combinations in the box.

away with	off with	up for	up with	out of
on with (x 2)	out with (x2)	up to	down on	

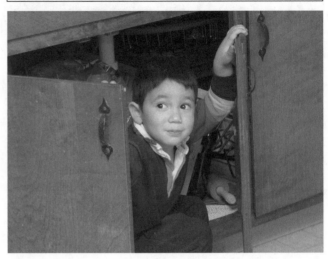

1. Joey! You've got a very guilty look on your face! What naughty things have you been getting **up to** this time?

2. The burglar broke into the house and made _____ a lot of jewellery.

3. We must try to cut _____ the amount of money we spend a month. We spend more than we earn.

4. Don't let me disturb you. Carry _____ your work.

5. I'm sorry we didn't get into the cinema. I'll take you to a restaurant to make _____ it. Does that cheer you up?

6. There is a move in Britain to do _____ the monarchy completely, so that Britain would become a republic.

7. Sam's mean with money, and he's always trying to get _____ paying his fair share of the bills for the flat.

8. I went _____ Aimee for two years, and then we broke up.

9. I can't put _____ Paul's rudeness a minute longer. I'm leaving him.

10. Judith is a very difficult person to get _____ . She's always falling _____ people.

Listening

9 Not getting on

1 🎧 Listen to the conversation and choose the best answer.

1 Sophie's upset about …
- a ☐ her friend.
- b ☐ the evening.
- c ☐ her boyfriend.

2 Charlie's …
- a ☐ ignored her.
- b ☐ been mean to her.
- c ☐ laughed at her.

3 Charlie's …
- a ☐ out of work.
- b ☐ having problems at work.
- c ☐ looking for a new job.

4 Anya wants Sophie to …
- a ☐ leave him.
- b ☐ be nice to him.
- c ☐ tell him to stop it.

5 Sophie …
- a ☐ agrees to this.
- b ☐ doesn't want to, because she loves him.
- c ☐ wants things to get magically better.

6 After talking to Anya, Sophie feels …
- a ☐ miserable.
- b ☐ more cheerful.
- c ☐ annoyed.

2 🎧 Listen again and complete these sentences.

Exaggeration and Understatement

1 You look _____ ! ☐

2 I'm just _____ , that's all. ☐

3 He made _____ remarks this evening. ☐

4 He's been having _____ at work recently. ☐

5 I think his behaviour is _____ . ☐

6 It's getting me _____ , I must say. ☐

7 I'm _____ him, you know. ☐

8 You sound _____ already! ☐

3 Which sentences from exercise 2 are examples of exaggeration (**E**) and which are understatement (**U**)?

Pronunciation

10 Consonant clusters

English has many words with groups (or clusters) of consonants:

happened	/hæpənd/
couldn't	/kʊdnt/
puzzles	/pʌzlz/

🎧 These words all have consonant clusters. Say them aloud and then transcribe them.

1 /dʌznt/ _____
2 /ʃʊdnt/ _____
3 /mʌsnt/ _____
4 /prɒmɪst/ _____
5 /ɒstreɪlɪə/ _____
6 /plæŋks/ _____
7 /ædəlesnt/ _____
8 /əreɪndʒd/ _____
9 /rɪleɪʃnʃɪp/ _____
10 /æŋgri/ _____
11 /ɪksaɪtmənt/ _____
12 /ɪmprest/ _____

11 Sentence stress

🎧 Rob and Stuart are chatting about Frank. Read the conversation aloud and mark the stress in Stuart's responses.

1	**Rob**	Don't you think Frank's put on a lot of weight recently?
	Stuart	You're kidding. If anything, he's lost weight.
2	**Rob**	I think Frank earns more than me.
	Stuart	Well, I know he earns a lot more than me.
3	**Rob**	He's thinking of buying a second-hand Mercedes.
	Stuart	What do you mean? He's already bought a brand new one.
4	**Rob**	He's just bought two pairs of designer jeans.
	Stuart	Didn't you know that all Frank's clothes are designer labels?
5	**Rob**	Does Frank have many stocks and shares?
	Stuart	He has loads of them.
6	**Rob**	Isn't Frank in New York on business?
	Stuart	No, in fact he's in Florida on holiday.
7	**Rob**	His latest girlfriend has long, blonde hair.
	Stuart	Really? The girl I saw him with had short, brown hair.

8

Relative clauses • Participles
• Adjectives • Nouns in groups • Adjectives and prepositions
• Silent consonants

How remarkable!

Defining and non-defining relative clauses

1 General knowledge quiz

Test your general knowledge. Tick (✔) the correct answer.

Remarkable things, people, and places

1 **The first video that reached one billion views on YouTube was**
   a ☐ the wedding of Prince William and Kate Middleton.
   b ☐ the Korean pop song 'Gangnam Style'.
   c ☐ Barack Obama's 2012 victory speech.

2 **The first woman**
   a ☐ who walked to the North Pole
   b ☐ who skied to the South Pole
   c ☐ who climbed Everest
   was Felicity Aston.

3 **A megacity is a city which has more than**
   a ☐ 10 million inhabitants.
   b ☐ 15 million inhabitants.
   c ☐ 20 million inhabitants.

4 **The Statue of Liberty, which was a gift from France to the USA,**
   a ☐ is the tallest statue in the world.
   b ☐ is the heaviest statue in the world.
   c ☐ is made from bronze.

5 **The most expensive hotel in the world, where a suite costs $81,000 a night,**
   a ☐ is Burj Al Arab, in Dubai.
   b ☐ is The Raj Palace Hotel, in Jaipur.
   c ☐ is Hotel President Wilson, in Geneva.

6 **Lewis Carroll,**
   a ☐ whose real name was Charles Lutwidge Dodgson,
   b ☐ whose real name was Clive Staples Lewis,
   c ☐ whose real name was Christopher James Dalton,
   wrote several famous poems and books, including
   Alice in Wonderland.

7 **Central Park, which is in New York City,**
   a ☐ is the most filmed location in the world.
   b ☐ is the largest urban park in the world.
   c ☐ is the smallest urban park in the world.

8 **The largest hot desert on Earth is the Sahara,**
   a ☐ which is 14 million square kilometres.
   b ☐ which is 4 million square kilometres.
   c ☐ which is 10 million square kilometres.

2 Defining or non-defining?

1 Decide if these sentences are best completed with a defining relative clause (D) or a non-defining relative clause (ND). Write **D** or **ND** in the boxes.

1 ☐ I'd love to meet someone _____ _____ .

2 ☐ We're looking for a house _____ _____ .

3 ☐ We went to see *Romeo and Juliet* _____ _____ .

4 ☐ Do you know a shop _____ _____ .

5 ☐ Marilyn Monroe _____ _____ died of a drug overdose.

6 ☐ I find people _____ difficult to get on with.

7 ☐ My computer _____ is already out of date.

8 ☐ I met a girl _____ .

9 ☐ Professor Brian Cox _____ will give a talk next week.

10 ☐ I bought a cheese and pickle sandwich _____ _____ .

2 Complete the sentences in exercise 1 with this information. Add a relative pronoun and commas where necessary. Leave out the relative pronoun if possible.

> You went to school with her.
>
> I ate it immediately.
>
> It has four bedrooms.
>
> I bought it only last year.
>
> They lose their temper easily.
>
> It sells second-hand furniture.
>
> Her real name was Norma Jean Baker.
>
> This person could teach me how to cook.
>
> He's a well-known physicist and TV presenter.
>
> I really enjoyed it.

3 Punctuation and omitting the pronoun

Add commas to these sentences if they have a non-defining relative clause. If possible, cross out the pronoun in the defining relative clauses.

1 Sheila**,** who I first got to know at university**,** was one of six children.

2 The man ~~who~~ you were talking to is a famous artist.

3 This is the story that amazed the world. (no change)

4 The thing that I most regret is not going to university.

5 My two daughters who are 16 and 13 are both interested in dancing.

6 The town where I was born has changed dramatically.

7 I didn't like the clothes which were in the sale.

8 The phone that I bought yesterday doesn't work.

9 The part of Europe where I'd most like to live is Portugal.

10 The Algarve where my mother's family comes from is famous for its beautiful beaches and dramatic coastline.

11 Salt that comes from the sea is considered to be the best for cooking.

12 Salt whose qualities have been known since prehistoric times is used to season and preserve food.

4 All relative pronouns

1 Match a line in **A** with a line in **B**.

A	B
1 Have I told you recently	a ☐ when you expect to arrive.
2 I have to do	b ☐ where my brother lives.
3 We were stuck in traffic for hours,	c ☐ which came as a bit of a surprise.
4 We're emigrating to Australia,	d ☐ whose body was covered in tattoos.
5 I met a girl	e ☑ how much I love you?
6 I passed all my exams,	f ☐ whatever you want.
7 Let me know	g ☐ which was a nightmare.
8 I'll buy you	h ☐ what I believe to be right.

2 Complete the sentences with a relative pronoun. If the pronoun can be omitted, add nothing.

1 The lady _____ is sitting in the wheelchair is my grandmother.

2 I know an Italian restaurant _____ serves excellent pasta.

3 I know an Italian restaurant _____ you can always get a table.

4 Uncle Tom earns a fortune, _____ is why I've asked him to lend me £1,000.

5 Sean is a child _____ people immediately like.

6 My daughter, _____ ambition is to emigrate to Australia, has finally got her visa.

7 I gave him a glass of water, _____ he drank thirstily.

8 The flight _____ we wanted to get was fully booked.

9 My auntie's house is the place _____ I feel most at home.

10 This is the smallest car _____ has ever been made.

11 That's the man _____ wife left him because he kept his pet snake in their bedroom.

12 I love the things _____ you say to me.

13 I go shopping at the new shopping centre, _____ there's always free parking.

14 She told me she'd been married before, _____ I hadn't realized.

15 _____ you do, don't touch that button. It turns off the power.

5 Prepositions in relative clauses

Combine the sentences, keeping the preposition after the verb in the relative clause.

1 I want you to meet the people. I work with them.

   I want you to meet the people I work with.

2 She's a friend. I can always rely on her.

   _____

   _____

3 That's the man. The police were looking for him.

   _____

   _____

4 She recommended a book by Robert Palmer. I'd never heard of him.

   _____

   _____

5 You paid £200 for a pair of trainers. They have been reduced to £100.

   The trainers _____

   _____

6 This is the book. I was telling you about it.

   _____

7 The Prime Minister gave a good speech. I agree with his views.

   _____

   _____

8 His talk was on the environment. I care deeply about this.

   _____

   _____

9 What's that music? You're listening to it.

   _____

   _____

10 My mother died last week. I looked after her for many years.

   _____

   _____

Participles

6 Participles as adjectives

Complete the adjectives with -ed or -ing.

1 a shock**ing** fact
2 a reserv**ed** seat
3 scream_____ babies
4 a satisfi_____ customer
5 a disgust_____ meal
6 a confus_____ explanation
7 a challeng_____ job
8 a conceit_____ person
9 a frighten_____ film
10 an exhaust_____ walk
11 a disappoint_____ outcome
12 a tir_____ journey
13 an unexpect_____ visit
14 disturb_____ images
15 a thrill_____ story
16 an amus_____ remark
17 a disappoint_____ customer
18 well-behav_____ children
19 a promis_____ start
20 a cake load_____ with calories

7 Participle clauses

1 Rewrite the sentences with a present or past participle clause instead of a relative clause.

1 Can you see the woman who's dressed in red over there?

<u>Can you see the woman dressed in red over there?</u>

2 People who live in blocks of flats often complain of loneliness.

_____

3 Letters that are posted before 5.00 p.m. should arrive the next day.

_____

4 The train that is standing on platform five is for Manchester.

_____

5 Firemen have rescued passengers who were trapped in the accident.

_____

6 They live in a lovely house that overlooks the River Thames.

_____

7 It took workmen days to clear up the litter that was dropped by the crowds.

_____

2 Complete the sentences with a verb from the box in either its present or past participle form.

| feel | borrow | explain | say | ~~ruin~~ | study | take | pass | steal |

1 My dad was in a bad mood for the whole week, completely **ruining** the holiday.

2 After _____ all her exams with A grades, Maggie went out to celebrate.

3 Jewellery _____ in the robbery has never been recovered.

4 I got a letter from the Tax Office _____ that I owe them £1,000.

5 _____ hungry, I decided to make myself a sandwich.

6 Books _____ from the library must be returned in two weeks.

7 I had a long talk to Ruby, _____ why it was important for her to work hard.

8 _____ everything into consideration, I've decided to give you a second chance.

9 With both children _____ at university, the house seems really quiet.

Relatives and participles review

8 Fearless Felix

Read and complete the article with the clauses in the box.

Relative clause
which has put him
that scared him
who jumped
what no man has done
whose skydiving career
from which he would leap
which can happen when
whose fear of being enclosed

Past participle
known as Fearless Felix
terrified of wearing

Present participle
including his mother and his girlfriend
knowing he had to

THE 24-MILE JUMP FROM SPACE

Felix Baumgartner, otherwise [1] _____, is the Austrian man [2] _____ from the edge of space and became the first man to break the speed of sound in free fall.

Baumgartner, [3] _____ spanned nearly two decades before he started training for his most daring skydive of all, was, understandably, afraid of the challenge. However, it wasn't the magnitude of the dive [4] _____ most, but rather the outfit he had to wear to travel through space.

The skydiver, [5] _____ was, incredibly, greater than his fear of doing the jump itself, had problems with the pressurized space suit. [6] _____ a suit that restricted his movement, and [7] _____ overcome his fear, Felix sought psychiatric help from a sports psychologist.

When he finally stood high above the Earth in the helium balloon, [8] _____ into space, he looked a solitary and vulnerable figure. There was every chance he could be falling into oblivion. At last, Felix jumped and immediately started to spin out of control, [9] _____ you travel at such a high speed. His 100-strong support team,

[10] _____, watched with their hearts in their mouths. However, Felix managed to stabilize himself and fulfill his dream. Baumgartner has done [11] _____ before: he has plummeted through 24 miles of cold, dark space at a speed of 843.6 miles per hour, a feat [12] _____ in *The Guinness Book of Records*.

Vocabulary

9 People, places, and things

1 Complete the table with these descriptive adjectives. There are six in each group.

unspoilt	stubborn	breathtaking	cracked	arrogant
humble	picturesque	automatic	conceited	handmade
loyal	waterproof	desolate	priceless	considerate
overcrowded	smashed	built-up		

People	Places	Things
	unspoilt	

2 Complete the sentences with an adjective from exercise 1.

1 The view from the top of the mountain was absolutely _____ .

2 He's always boasting about how great he is at everything. He's so _____ .

3 Our new car is fully _____ . I don't want to change gears when I'm driving any more.

4 He is so kind and _____; he's always going out of his way to help people.

5 The countryside was completely _____ – rolling hills and green fields for miles around.

6 The Cotswolds is an area in England which is very _____ . It has lots of pretty, old-fashioned villages.

7 He's really _____ . He won't do a thing they tell him.

8 That bag you're looking at is _____ by local craftsmen. Look at the quality of the work.

9 The beach was seriously _____ . There was no room to put our towels down.

10 Nouns in groups

Look at these examples of number + noun + noun.
a three-mile walk
a 16-year-old girl
a ten-hour flight
These are expressions of measurement before a noun.
The number and the first noun are joined with a hyphen, and the first noun is usually in the singular.

Put the information before the noun.

1 a note that is worth ten pounds
_____

2 a language course that lasts eight weeks
_____

3 a drive that takes six hours
_____

4 a meal that consists of three courses
_____

5 a holiday that lasts one month
_____

6 a delay at the airport that went on for four hours
_____

7 a document that has 100 pages
_____

8 a university course that takes three years
_____

9 a prison sentence of ten years
_____

10 a hotel with five stars
_____

11 a speed limit of 30 mph
_____

12 a house that is 200 years old
_____

Prepositions

11 Adjective + preposition

Complete these sentences with the correct preposition.

1 Are you afraid _____ the dark?

2 She was angry _____ me _____ not telling her the news.

3 Canterbury is famous _____ its cathedral.

4 Bill is jealous _____ me because I'm so much cleverer than him.

5 I'm very proud _____ my two daughters.

6 I'm disappointed _____ you. I thought I could trust you.

7 You're very different _____ your brother. I thought you'd be similar _____ each other.

8 Are you excited _____ going on holiday?

9 Visitors to Britain aren't used _____ driving on the left.

10 Visitors to hot countries need to be aware _____ the risk of malaria.

11 You should be ashamed _____ what you did.

12 I am most grateful _____ all your help.

13 Who is responsible _____ this mess?

14 What's wrong _____ you? You don't look well.

15 My son is crazy _____ a band called *Moones*.

Pronunciation

12 Silent consonants

1 English words often have silent consonants:

k̶n̶o̶w̶   ̶w̶r̶i̶t̶e̶r̶   ̶w̶a̶l̶k̶   ̶c̶l̶i̶m̶b̶

🎧 Complete the table with these words. Cross out the silent consonants.

i̶n̶d̶u̶s̶t̶r̶y̶	honest	executive	inhabitant
r̶e̶c̶e̶i̶p̶t̶	distinctly	rebuilt	fasten
eccentric	insect	lamp	sumptuous
exhausted	whistle	straight	anonymous
citizen	fascinating	delighted	documentary
landscape	temperature	business	debt

Silent consonants	No silent consonants
receipt	industry

2 🎧 Write these words. They all have silent consonants.

1 /siːn/ _____   6 /ˈfraɪtnd/ _____

2 /saɪˈkaɪətrɪst/ _____   7 /ˈklaɪmə/ _____

3 /ˈhænsəm/ _____   8 /ˈgrænfɑːðə/ _____

4 /ˈaɪlənd/ _____   9 /ˈnɒlɪdʒ/ _____

5 /ˈkrɪsməs/ _____   10 /kɑːm/ _____

Expressing habit • *get* and *be* • Homonyms and homophones
• Phrasal verbs and nouns that go together • Weak and strong forms

The way we were

Present and past habit

1 Present habit

Match a sentence in **A** with a sentence in **B**.

A	B
1 She's really generous.	a ☐ She **jogs** to work every day.
2 He's so disorganized.	b ☐ They **get** everything they ask for.
3 She's very fashionable.	c ☐ She **never thinks** before she speaks.
4 He's so dishonest.	d ☐ He **never plans** anything properly.
5 She's so sensitive.	e ☐ He**'s always applying** for new jobs.
6 He's really stubborn.	f ☐ He**'s always telling** lies.
7 She's so rude.	g ☐ She**'s always buying** me presents.
8 They're so spoilt.	h ☐ She**'ll** only **wear** designer clothes.
9 She's very energetic.	i ☐ She**'ll start** crying at the slightest thing.
10 He's very ambitious.	j ☐ He **won't** ever **change** his mind.

2 My family's bad habits

Rewrite the sentences in one or two ways using *will/ won't* and/or the Present Continuous.

1 My dad mends his motorbike in the living room.

a _____

b _____

2 My brother leaves the top off the toothpaste.

a _____

b _____

3 He doesn't help with the household chores.

a _____

4 My sister borrows my clothes without asking.

a _____

b _____

5 My grandpa doesn't let anyone choose what's on TV.

a _____

6 My grandma gossips about the neighbours.

a _____

b _____

7 Carole and Alan boast about their children.

a _____

b _____

3 Past habit – used to

Complete the sentences with the correct form of *used to*: positive, question, or negative.

1 My grandfather never _____ get so out of breath when he climbed the stairs.
2 There _____ be a beautiful old building where that car park is now.
3 _____ have a Saturday job when you were at school?
4 She _____ be so moody. It's only since she lost her job.
5 _____ play cricket when you were at school?
6 Julie _____ be as slim as she is now. She's been dieting.
7 Where _____ go out to eat when you lived in Madrid?
8 _____ smoke 60 cigarettes a day? How did you give up?

4 It's so annoying!

Tick (✔) the sentences where the speaker is annoyed by someone's behaviour.

1 ☐ He watches sports programmes on TV.
   ☐ He's always watching sports programmes on TV.
2 ☐ She'd give us extra lessons after school.
   ☐ She *would* give us extra lessons after school.
   ☐ She was always giving us homework.
   ☐ She used to give us homework.
3 ☐ Our cat always used to sleep on my bed.
   ☐ Our cat would always sleep on *my* bed.
   ☐ Our cat always slept on my bed.
4 ☐ My boss is always asking me to stay late.
   ☐ My boss often asks me to stay late.
5 ☐ My children don't help out at home.
   ☐ My children will never help out at home.

5 used to and would

Which of the verb forms can complete the sentences below? Tick (✔) all possible answers.

1 I _____ long blonde hair when I was first married.
   a ✔ had **b** ✔ used to have **c** ☐ would have
2 We _____ every summer with our cousins in Scotland.
   a ☐ spent **b** ☐ used to spend **c** ☐ would spend
3 Pam _____ out with Andy for six months but then she ditched him.
   a ☐ went **b** ☐ used to go **c** ☐ would go
4 We _____ coffee and croissants every morning for breakfast.
   a ☐ had **b** ☐ used to have **c** ☐ would have
5 We _____ to each other every day when we were apart.
   a ☐ wrote **b** ☐ used to write **c** ☐ would write
6 He _____ to me for 20 years and then stopped.
   a ☐ wrote **b** ☐ used to write **c** ☐ would write
7 In the old days, people _____ you if you were in trouble.
   a ☐ helped **b** ☐ used to help **c** ☐ would help
8 I _____ living so close to the sea.
   a ☐ loved **b** ☐ used to love **c** ☐ would love
9 Dave _____ Molly three times if she wanted to go out with him.
   a ☐ asked **b** ☐ used to ask **c** ☐ would ask
10 I _____ questions in class. I was too shy.
   a ☐ never asked **b** ☐ never used to ask
   c ☐ would never ask
11 Before I worked here, I _____ as an assistant manager at a restaurant.
   a ☐ worked **b** ☐ used to work **c** ☐ would would
12 When I was a child, I _____ hours helping my mother in the garden.
   a ☐ often spent **b** ☐ often used to spend
   c ☐ would often spend

6 get and be

1 *Get used to* means *become used to* and describes a change of state. *Be used to* describes a state. Compare these sentences.

> Don't worry. You'll soon **get used to** working such long hours.
>
> I'm **used to** working long hours. I've done it for years.
>
> He eventually **got used to** the tropical climate, but it took a long time.
>
> He was born in India, so he's **used to** a hot climate.

2 *Get* + adjective usually means *become*.

> The sea's **getting rough**. Let's go back!

3 *Get* + past participle can be used to describe things we do to ourselves. It can also be used to describe things that happen to us, often negative events. Compare these sentences.

> I **got dressed** and went to work.
>
> We **got married** last week.
>
> I **got lost** on the mountain.

4 *Get* + infinitive can mean *have the opportunity to do something*. It can also describe a gradual change. Compare these sentences.

> She'll be furious if she **gets to hear** about this.
>
> As I **got to know** Paris, I started to like it more and more.

---

1 Complete the sentences with *used to*, *be used to*, or *get used to* in the correct form, positive or negative.

1 If you _____ Indian food, this dish might be too spicy for you.

2 I'll never _____ your hair that short. You'll have to grow it again.

3 **A** How do you drive in all this traffic?

   B I _____ it now, so it's OK. But it took me a while to _____ it, believe me!

4 Tom didn't like his new school at first, but he eventually _____ it, and made new friends.

5 I _____ jog every morning, but I don't any more. I'm so unfit now.

6 When I was a boy, I _____ like going to piano lessons, so I stopped. Now I'm in my forties, I've started learning again!

7 Sally won't find it easy to live on her own. She _____ her parents doing everything for her.

8 **A** I hate my new job!

   B Give it a chance. You may _____ it after you've been there a bit longer.

9 'Grandad, _____ you really _____ watch TV in black and white when you were young?'

10 **A** _____ you _____ your new teacher yet? I know you didn't like her much at first.

   B Well, I have a bit. She's OK, I suppose.

2 Complete the sentences with *get* or *be* in the correct form and a word or expression from the box.

| better | ready (x 2) | dressed | dark | tired |
| to know | a pilot | lost | upset | engaged |

1 I often _____ when I watch the news. Such awful things are happening in the world.

2 **A** How are you feeling?

   B I _____ slowly, but I still feel weak.

3 My little nephew is determined _____ when he grows up.

4 **A** Come on, Helen! The play starts in half an hour.

   B I _____ in two minutes. I _____ just _____ and putting my shoes on.

   A I don't know why it takes you so long. I _____ since 6.00.

5 **A** Do we turn right or left at the next junction?

   B I've no idea! I think we _____ .

6 **A** Did you hear that Sue and Chris _____ ?

   B No! I never thought they would!

7 I didn't use to like Mick at all, but the more I _____ him, the more I like him. Now he's my best friend!

8 In summer, it is still light at 9.00 in the evening, but in winter, it _____ at 5.00.

7 The day we met

1 Read the story. Which of the verbs in italics … ?

    a   … can change to both *used to* or *would*

    b   … can change only to *used to*

    c   … must stay in the Past Simple

    Write **a**, **b**, or **c** next to the verbs

Punk love

by Serena Fraser

It was the summer of '76. I was 15, and I was sunbathing in a local park when I [1] **c** *looked* up and saw the strangest-looking person. I [2] _____ *wore* flared trousers, mini-skirts, and flowery shirts like most teenagers, but this guy [3] _____ *looked* like he'd just landed from another planet. He [4] _____ *had* a spiky, blue Mohican, and despite the heat, he [5] _____ *was* dressed from head to toe in black leather! I was fascinated, so I [6] _____ *went* to the park regularly just to catch a glimpse of him. He and his friends [7] _____ *hung out* there most days. They [8] _____ *wore* a lot of make-up, even the boys, and their hair [9] _____ *changed* colour all the time! One day, he [10] _____ *spotted* me and [11] _____ *beckoned* me over. He [12] _____ *looked* so scary with his now green hair and black make-up, but I really wanted to meet him, so I [13] _____ *walked* over to say 'Hi'.

His name was Alan, he was 17, and he [14] _____ *studied* art at the local college. Even though he [15] _____ *dressed* weirdly, he was really interesting. I [16] _____ *spent* all my free time with him after that. We [17] _____ *met* in the park, or at the Bel café if we [18] _____ *had* any money, and we [19] _____ *talked* about art, music, politics, and all kinds of things. I [20] _____ *started* to dress like him and his friends, and Alan [21] _____ *came* with me when I got my first Mohican and [22] _____ *became* a proper punk! He [23] _____ *took* me to see lots of great punk bands like The Clash and the Sex Pistols. Alan [24] _____ *sang* in a band called Social Misfits, and he [25] _____ *pranced* about on stage like a mad thing. We [26] _____ *loved* going to gigs all over London.

We [27] _____ *got married* in 1980, dressed in black leather. Our three children [28] _____ *giggled* over our wedding photos, never quite believing that their parents [29] _____ *were* punks. We're quite normal-looking nowadays, but we still wear our black leather jackets to remind ourselves we weren't always middle-aged!

2 Complete these sentences about the story with one suitable word from the box.

got   used   wasn't   would

1 Serena often _____ to go to the park.

2 She _____ go just to see the weird-looking guy.

3 He and his friends _____ to wear a lot of make-up and dye their hair.

4 Serena _____ used to seeing men wearing make-up. She thought it strange.

5 However, she soon _____ used to the way they looked.

6 She _____ to know Alan very well.

7 She _____ to meet him regularly, and they _____ go for a coffee.

8 She got _____ to listening to punk music. She _____ to like it.

Vocabulary

8 Homonyms

Use the same word to complete each pair of sentences.

1 **a** The sun <u>rose</u> brightly over the house this morning.

   b He's very romantic. He always gives me a red <u>rose</u> when we go on a date.

2 **a** Look out of the window, Josie – there's Daddy coming up the path! _____ to him!

   b With each huge _____, the ferry rocked, and I began to feel really sick.

3 **a** Look, I've no idea what you're arguing about. What _____ are you trying to make?

   b He couldn't speak the language, so he just used to _____ whenever he wanted something.

4 **a** Everyone has the _____ to a fair trial.

   b Well done! You got all the answers _____ in the test.

5 **a** Gosh, you look smart! Is that a new _____ and tie you're wearing?

   b Well, I think you should buy the pale green dress. The red one doesn't _____ you.

6 **a** See the man with blue eyes and _____ hair? That's Jenny's husband.

   b It's not _____ ! You gave him more than me!

7 **a** Oh, look! Justin Bieber's on at the Palladium. Can we get tickets? I'm a real _____ of his.

   b It's boiling hot. Could we switch the _____ on and get some air circulating?

8 **a** He noticed the thin gold _____ on her ring finger.

   b He used to play in a rock _____ in his youth.

9 Homophones

Write the correct spelling of the words in phonetics.

▶ **Phonetic symbols p100**

1 **a** I'm /bɔːd/! I can't think of anything to do.

   b He jumped on his surf /bɔːd/ and paddled out to the biggest waves.

   a _____ b _____

2 **a** Stop it! You know you aren't /əlaʊd/ to do that!

   b Michael, please stand up and read your story /əlaʊd/ to the class.

   a _____ b _____

3 **a** She was happy to get her bag back when the police /kɔːt/ the thief.

   b The thief was sentenced to three months in prison at /kɔːt/ the next day.

   a _____ b _____

4 **a** Sara took out a /ləʊn/ to pay for her university course.

   b The bad weather prevented us from climbing any further, but we could see one /ləʊn/ climber on the summit.

   a _____ b _____

5 **a** We looked for a car /haɪə/ place in our holiday resort so that we could travel around a bit.

   b Throw the ball /haɪə/ or you'll never get it in the basket!

   a _____ b _____

Q What sort of crisps can fly?

A Plain crisps.

Patient Doctor, I keep thinking I'm a billiard ball.

Doctor Go to the end of the cue.

Phrasal verbs

10 Phrasal verbs and nouns that go together

1 Some phrasal verbs have a strong association with certain objects: *set out on a journey*; *work out the solution to a problem*.

Match a verb with an object. There may be more than one answer, but there is one that is best.

1	come up with	a	☐	someone you respect
2	break into	b	☐	a naughty child
3	break off	c	☐	a problem, a complaint, a difficult customer
4	tell off	d	☐	the other people in the group
5	bring up	e	☐	a university course after one year
6	count on	f	☐	a solution to a problem
7	deal with	g	☐	your best friend to help you
8	drop out of	h	☐	children to be honest and hard-working
9	fit in with	i	☐	a house or a flat, to steal something
10	look up to	j	☐	a fact that someone might not be aware of
11	point out	k	☐	what I said – I didn't mean it
12	take back	l	☐	a relationship, an engagement

2 Complete the sentences with the correct form of a phrasal verb from exercise 1.

1 The thieves _____ the warehouse and stole goods worth £20,000.

2 He _____ his elder sister because she always seemed so wise and experienced.

3 I accused you of being mean the other day. I _____ it all _____ . I'm sorry.

4 I hadn't noticed that the living room was a different colour until someone _____ it _____ to me.

5 Scientists will have to _____ new methods of increasing the world's food supply.

6 She _____ Tom _____ because he hit his sister.

7 You have a problem with your order, madam? I'll just get someone to _____ it for you.

8 I had a new student today. He seems very nice. I'm sure he'll _____ the rest of the class just fine.

9 Why did you _____ university after just one term? What are you going to do now?

10 I'm running for President. I hope I can _____ your support.

11 My parents _____ me _____ to finish all the food on my plate.

12 It was never going to work, so Marie and Jim decided to _____ their engagement.

Listening

11 A small disagreement

1 🎧 Listen to the conversation between a young couple, Megan and Harry. Mark these statements true (✔) or false (✗). Correct the false ones.

1 They are arguing about a film they have seen. ☐

2 They would both often watch TV talent shows when they were at university. ☐

3 These programmes always used to make them cry. ☐

4 Megan believes that the format of these shows has become too predictable. ☐

5 Last year's winner was a girl called Ella with an amazing voice. ☐

6 Harry takes these shows very seriously. ☐

7 Megan thinks it's time Harry acted his age. ☐

8 Megan persuades Harry to watch a film with her. ☐

2 🎧 Look at the phrases in bold that Megan and Harry use to make their points. Listen again and complete the lines from their conversation.

1 **If you want my opinion**, it's _____, over the top, and _____ predictable.

2 **The problem now is that** it's the same _____ format.

3 **I don't agree that** it's a _____ .

4 **The point I'm trying to make** is that most of them _____ !

5 **If you ask me**, you're _____ off watching a good film.

6 **To tell you the truth**, I don't mind being _____ .

7 **I know what you say is true**, but I _____ .

8 **The main point** is not to take it too _____ , which you _____ do.

Pronunciation

12 Weak and strong forms

🎧 Auxiliary verbs have weak and strong forms, depending on whether they are unstressed or stressed.

1 Sometimes the weak form is a contraction.

he is = he's

she does not = she doesn't

I have not = I haven't

2 Sometimes the weak form is a change in the vowel sound. This is often a change to /ə/.

	Weak	Strong
was	/wəz/ *Was Tom there?*	/wɒz/ *Yes, he was.*
were	/wə/ *Were you there?*	/wɜː/ *Yes, we were.*
can	/kən/ *Can you swim?*	/kæn/ (can't = /kɑːnt/) *Yes, I can.*
been	/bɪn/ *I've been shopping*	/biːn/ *Where have you been?*

Some prepositions also have weak and strong vowel sounds.

	Weak	Strong		Weak	Strong
to	/tə/	/tuː/	for	/fə/	/fɔː/
of	/əv/	/ɒv/	from	/frəm/	/frɒm/
at	/ət/	/æt/			

1 🎧 Listen and circle all the weak vowel sounds in the sentences. Underline all those with strong vowels

1 I don't want to see him but I'm sure you want to.

2 Sue isn't going to learn from the experience, but Tom is.

3 I've heard that you're thinking of moving from London. Are you?

4 They have dinner at seven, don't they?

5 You'll be able to get a ticket for me, won't you?

6 I've got no idea who this letter's from.

7 Can't you remember who Bill used to work for?

8 I've been waiting for you to come. Where were you?

9 We'd been looking forward to coming for ages, then at the last minute we weren't able to.

10 Won't you sit down for a couple of minutes?

2 Read the telephone conversation between two friends and transcribe **A**'s lines. Add punctuation to make the meaning clear.

▶▶ **Phonetic symbols p100**

A /wɒt ə jə duːɪŋ ət ðə wiːkend/ ?

What are you doing at the weekend?

B I haven't decided yet.

A /wɪə gəʊɪŋ tə skɒtlənd djə wɒntə kʌm tuː/ ?

_____

_____

B I'd love to. Where are you staying?

A /wiv dɪsaɪdɪd tə kæmp nʌn əv əs kən əfɔːd tə peɪ fərə həʊtel/

_____

_____

B Camping in Scotland in October! You'll be freezing cold.

A /nəʊ wi wəʊnt wiv gɒt strɒŋ tents lɒts əv wɔːm kləʊz ən θɪk sliːpɪŋ bægz/

_____

_____

B Have you checked the weather forecast?

A /əv kɔːs wi hæv ən ɪts prɪti wɔːm fər ɒktəʊbə/

_____

_____

B OK then. It'll be quite an adventure!

A /eksələnt aɪl tel ði ʌðəz ðeɪl bi dɪlaɪtəd wiːl pɪk juː ʌp ət sɪks ɒn fraɪdeɪ siː juː ðen gʊdbaɪ/

_____

_____

B Bye!

🎧 Listen and check.

10

Modal auxiliary verbs in the past • Body idioms
• Verbs + prepositions • Rhymes and limericks

Over my dead body!

Revision of modals

1 Present to past

Rewrite the sentences to make them refer to the past.

1 I must read *Richard III* before my course begins.

   I had to read Richard III before my course began.

2 I have to take the pills three times a day.

   _____
   _____

3 They must be away on holiday.

   _____

4 We can't have a lunch break – there's too much to do!

   _____
   _____

5 He can't be a millionaire.

   _____

6 We mustn't shout in the classroom.

   _____
   _____

7 He won't go to bed.

   _____

8 That will be John on the phone.

   _____

9 You should be more careful.

   _____

10 You could help with the washing-up for a change.

   _____
   _____

Modal verbs of probability

2 How certain?

1 Decide on the degree of certainty in these sentences. Put two ticks (✔✔) if the idea expressed is certain. Put one tick (✔) if it is less certain.

1 [✔✔] You must have seen him at the cinema. I know he was there.
2 [✔] The dog is really dirty. He might have been swimming in the lake.
3 [ ] He can't have been telling the truth.
4 [ ] He might have left a message on your mobile.
5 [ ] I don't know where she is. She may have gone shopping.
6 [ ] She must have been very upset when you told her the news.
7 [ ] They're not answering their phone. They must have gone away already.
8 [ ] I don't see their car. They can't have come back yet.
9 [ ] It's six o'clock. Tom will have gone home by now.
10 [ ] Matthew isn't here – he might have thought you weren't coming and gone to the cinema by himself.
11 [ ] I could have cancelled the meeting if I'd known earlier!
12 [ ] Ian will be back soon. It's Friday. He'll have gone to the pub after work.

🎧 Listen and notice the stress and intonation.

2 Make sentences from the table.

If I go to Norway, I If I went to Norway, I If I'd gone to Norway, I	can will may might would could	see the fjords. have seen the fjords.

1 _____
2 _____
3 _____
4 _____
5 _____
6 _____

3 Past probability

1 Write sentences for the situations below, using the information in the box.

		cut it	a cake.
		gone	a party last night.
		mislaid	to Andy.
He	must have	arrived home	something naughty.
She	can't have	got engaged	for ages.
They	might have	had	without me.
		been doing	by now.
		been making	my number.

1 Stella's wearing a beautiful diamond ring.

_____

_____

2 The children ran away laughing and giggling.

_____

_____

3 There's flour on grandma's nose.

_____

_____

4 Paulo and Geri said they'd wait for me, but I can't see them.

_____

_____

5 Tim's flat is so clean and tidy.

_____

_____

6 It's after midnight. Henri and Sally left ages ago.

_____

_____

7 I don't know why Tara didn't ring.

_____

_____

8 Look at Joe's hair. It's really long!

_____

_____

2 Write sentences for the situations below using the information in the box in the perfect infinitive passive.

		washed	by the wind.
It		hit	by a stone.
It	must have been	blown down	properly.
They	can't have been	repaired	recently.
		dry-cleaned	with something red.

1 A tree has fallen across the road.

_____

_____

2 My white jeans have turned pink!

_____

_____

3 My TV has broken and I've only just had it fixed.

_____

_____

4 David's suit looks a bit dirty.

_____

_____

5 The car windscreen has shattered.

_____

_____

Ruby must have eaten it.

4 Past modals of deduction

Complete the conversations with the correct form of the verbs in brackets.

1 **A** I wonder how the thief got into our apartment?

  B He [1] _____ (could / use) the fire escape or he [2] _____ (might / climb up) that tree.

  A Well, he [3] _____ (need not / bother). There's nothing to steal!

2 **A** Bill told me that he'd spent £2,000 on a birthday present for his girlfriend, but he [4] _____ (must / joke). Surely he [5] _____ (can not / spend) that much.

  B I think you [6] _____ (might / mishear) him!

3 **A** It's 3.30. Mum and Dad's plane landed over an hour ago. They [7] _____ (should / phone)!

  B They [8] _____ (may / be delayed). No, look! They're driving up now. You [9] _____ (need not / worry).

4 **A** You're very sunburnt. You [10] _____ (would not / burn) if you'd used your factor 30 suncream.

  B I [11] _____ (must / fall) asleep. And I [12] _____ (can not / put on) enough cream. Ouch!

5 Past modals – revision of all modal verbs

(Circle) the correct answer.

1 I'm sorry. I *shouldn't have / couldn't have* told Tom what you said about him.

2 **A** Where's the dog?
  B Don't know. Dad *may have / 'll have* taken him for a walk.
  A No. I remember. It's Tuesday, isn't it? Mum *should have / 'll have* taken him to the vet.

3 **A** Are Pat and Jan definitely coming? I'*d have / might have* thought they'd have arrived by now.
  B They *should have / could have* been held up by traffic, don't you think?
  A Or they *might have / needn't have* had an accident!
  B Don't be silly. Anyway, we'*d have / must have* heard by now if something like that had happened.
  A Well, I *needn't have / mustn't have* prepared lunch so early. And I think they *should have / may have* rung if they knew they were going to be late.

4 **A** Who was that man?
  B He *can't have / must have* been a friend of Jane's. He was asking if I'd seen her.

Conman
Canoe man

John Darwin claimed it [1] _could not have been_ (can not/be) easier to fake his own death and get away with it, but returning from the dead is not so easy! He now says he [2] _____ never _____ (should /come back).

6 Canoe Death Hoax

1 Complete the article, putting the modals and verbs in brackets in the past.

2 Are the sentences true (✓) or false (✗)?

  1 ☐ John said it was difficult to fake your own death.

  2 ☐ The Emergency Services thought that currents had dragged John's body out to sea.

  3 ☐ John's wife wasn't involved in the insurance fraud.

  4 ☐ The police caught John and Anne in Panama five years later.

  5 ☐ The couple's two sons had no idea that their father was alive.

  6 ☐ The police never believed that the sons were involved in the insurance fraud.

  7 ☐ John does not regret his actions.

  8 ☐ John wishes he had stayed in Panama.

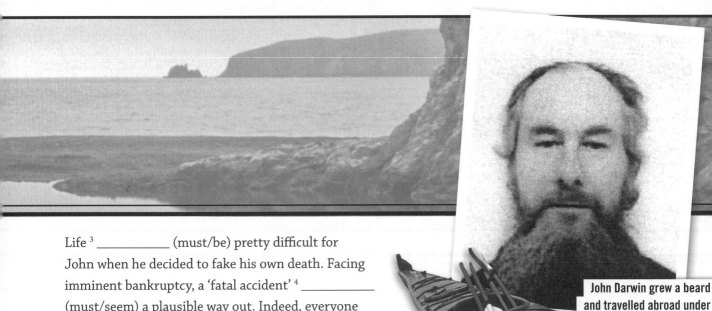

John Darwin grew a beard and travelled abroad under the name of John Jones.

Life ³ _____ (must/be) pretty difficult for John when he decided to fake his own death. Facing imminent bankruptcy, a 'fatal accident' ⁴ _____ (must/seem) a plausible way out. Indeed, everyone believed that he had accidentally fallen from his canoe into the sea near his home in County Durham. Even the Emergency Services said John ⁵ _____ (can not/survive) the strong currents which ⁶ _____ certainly _____ (would/drag) his body out to sea, never to be recovered.

No one ⁷ _____ (could/imagine) that John was very much alive and well, and living off his £680,000 life insurance money with his wife, Anne, in Panama. However, John's conscience ⁸ _____ (must/get)

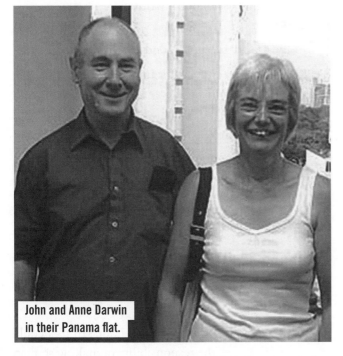

John and Anne Darwin in their Panama flat.

the better of him as five years after his disappearance, he walked into a police station in London claiming to have lost his memory.

At first, the police mistakenly assumed the Darwins' sons ⁹ _____ (must/involve) in the scam, and they ¹⁰ _____ (might/received) prison sentences. But John and Anne insisted that their two sons had not known their father was really alive. When they realized both their parents ¹¹ _____ (must/lie) to them for over four years, they were appalled.

Asked how he ¹² _____ (could/put) his own children through the trauma of thinking he had drowned, John admits that he ¹³ _____ (might not/act) in their best interests, but that he had been extremely stressed.

He said, 'I ¹⁴ _____ (should not/commit) the crime, and I ¹⁵ _____ (should not/come back)'.

John has been accused of not showing enough remorse, but he is very philosophical. He says, 'If you don't believe it, you don't believe it!'

Vocabulary

7 Body idioms

Complete the conversations with the correct body idiom from the box.

heart-to-heart	enter your head	all fingers and thumbs
all ears	face the facts	put on a brave face
cold feet	give me a hand	hands full
out of my mind		

1
Mary Oops! Oh Clare, I'm really sorry! I've just broken your pink coffee cup. I'm ¹ _____ today.

Clare Oh, never mind. It can't be helped.

2
Jane I had a real ² _____ with Emily and told her exactly what we thought about her new boyfriend.

Diane Oooh! That was brave. What did you say exactly? Go on, tell me. I'm ³ _____ .

Jane That he was a lazy waste of space, and she should stop seeing him.

3
Dad It's nearly midnight and I've been ⁴ _____ with worry. Where have you been young lady?

Jo Sorry, Dad! The taxi was late bringing us back from the party.

Dad Did it never ⁵ _____ to ring or at least text me?

4
Nick Hi, Jake. What's up with you? Are you alright?

Jake Well, I was supposed to be giving a talk to my English class, and at the last minute I got ⁶ _____ , and I just couldn't do it.

Nick Don't worry. We all get nervous about things like that.

5
Fiona Josh, can you ⁷ _____ with my English assignment? I really don't understand what I'm meant to be doing?

Josh Sorry, Fiona, I've got my ⁸ _____ at the moment. I've only just started writing my history essay which has to be handed in tomorrow.

6
Tina You've just got to ⁹ _____ , Julie. Your marriage is over. You can't keep on finding excuses for Rob's bad behaviour.

Julie Don't you think I should just ¹⁰ _____ for the children's sake and give him one more chance?

Tina No, I don't. Enough is enough!

🎧 Listen and check.

8 Physical appearance or personality?

1 Write these adjectives in the correct columns. Careful! One adjective can go in both columns.

~~skinny~~	moody	big-headed
brainy	graceful	wrinkled
quick-thinking	nosy	bald
cheeky	well-built	narrow-minded
affectionate	smart	curly
hard-hearted	clean-shaven	tanned

Physical appearance	Personality
skinny	

2 Complete the sentences with the parts of the body in the box, used as verbs.

arm	elbow	eye	foot	hand	head	shoulder	thumb

1 The teacher _____ out the exam papers and told the class to begin writing.

2 I managed to _____ my way to the front of the crowd, so I got a good view of the procession.

3 I haven't read the magazine yet, I just _____ through it to see if there were any interesting pictures.

4 We all _____ the new member of class with curiosity. We were eager to see what she was like.

5 They ordered the most expensive things on the menu because they knew that I'd _____ the bill.

6 In the final seconds of the match, Benson _____ the ball into the back of the net, making it 1–0.

7 Policemen _____ with guns in some countries.

8 I'd hate to be Prime Minister. I don't think I could _____ the responsibility of making so many important decisions.

Prepositions

9 Verb + preposition

Complete the sentences with a verb in its correct form and a preposition.

Verbs		Prepositions	
thank	forgive	into	of
accuse	hide	at	on
trick	hold	for	to
congratulate	inherit	from	
shout	model		
invite	remind		

1 He __thanked__ the nurse __for__ all her help.

2 You _____ me so much _____ your father. You look just like him.

3 Everyone _____ me _____ passing my driving test at the fourth attempt.

4 My teenage daughter _____ herself _____ her pop idol. She's had a ring put through her nose, just like him.

5 Don't _____ the truth _____ me. I want to know everything.

6 He picked up the crying baby and _____ her tightly _____ his chest.

7 We've _____ 300 guests _____ our wedding.

8 I think that TV ads _____ people _____ buying things that they don't really want.

9 I didn't _____ a penny _____ my great uncle when he died.

10 The spectators _____ abuse _____ the referee when he disallowed the goal.

11 How can I ever _____ him _____ telling me all those lies?

12 I _____ by my employers _____ stealing, which I strongly denied.

Pronunciation

10 Rhymes and limericks

1 Make rhyming pairs with the words from the box.

good	chief	court	deaf	fool	mud
height	lose	knew	knows	grieve	put
reign	nude	said	pour	weight	wool

should /ʊd/ __good__   food /uːd/ _____

bread /ed/ _____   leaf /iːf/ _____

choose /uːz/ _____   taught /ɔːt/ _____

toes /əʊz/ _____   chef /ef/ _____

hate /eɪt/ _____   through /uː/ _____

tight /aɪt/ _____   wore /ɔː/ _____

full /ʊl/ _____   brain /eɪn/ _____

pool /uːl/ _____   leave /iːv/ _____

blood /ʌd/ _____   foot /ʊt/ _____

2 Limericks are short poems with a distinctive rhythm. The lines rhyme AABBA. Transcribe the lines written in phonetics in these two limericks.

The Pelican

A rare old bird is a pelican

His /biːk kən həʊld mɔː ðən ɪz beli kaːn/

_____

He /kən teɪk ɪn hɪz biːk/

_____

/ɪnʌf fuːd fər ə wiːk/

_____

And I'm damned if I know how the hell he can!

The Lady from Twickenham

There was a young lady from Twickenham

Whose /ʃuːz wə tuː taɪt tə wɔːk kwɪk ɪn ðəm/

_____

She came back from a walk

/lʊkɪŋ waɪtə ðən tʃɔːk/

_____

And she /tʊk ðəm bəʊθ ɒf ən wəz sɪk ɪn ðəm/

_____

11

Hypothesizing • Wishes and regrets • *unless, supposing, in case*
• Similar words, different meanings • Nouns from phrasal verbs
• Ways of pronouncing *ea*

It's all hypothetical!

Real time or unreal time?

1 Real or hypothetical past?

1 These sentences all have verbs in the Past Simple. Which refer to real past time (**R**) and which are hypotheses (**H**)?

1 R Did you see Lorenzo when you were in Italy?
2 H I wish I worked in the open air.
3 ☐ If you didn't have a car, would you have to go by bus?
4 ☐ When we lived in London, we'd always travel by bus.
5 ☐ I'd rather we lived in a small country town.
6 ☐ It's time we had a new sofa.
7 ☐ If only you were always as happy as you are today.
8 ☐ Why didn't you come to the party?

2 These sentences all have verbs in the Past Perfect. Which refer to real past time (**R**) and which are hypotheses (**H**)?

1 ☐ I wish I'd said that.
2 ☐ She asked me if I had known him for a long time.
3 ☐ If I hadn't been in a meeting, I'd have taken your call.
4 ☐ If only you'd arrived five minutes earlier.
5 ☐ I woke up and realized it had all been a terrible dream.
6 ☐ What if they hadn't agreed to give you a pay rise?
7 ☐ Had the water risen a bit more, our house would have been flooded.
8 ☐ She told me she'd been given a kitten for her birthday.

3 Complete the sentences with an auxiliary verb which expresses reality.

1 I wish you didn't bite your nails, but you **do** .
2 I wish I earned more, but I _____ .
3 I should have listened to their advice, but I _____ .
4 If only I could speak Spanish, but I _____ .
5 If only he weren't so selfish, but he _____ .
6 I wish my car would start, but it _____ .
7 I wish he didn't argue all the time, but he _____ .
8 If only I hadn't been fired, but I _____ .
9 I wish I had a flat of my own, but I _____ .

Wishes and regrets

2 Present and past wishes

1 Use the words from the columns to make as many correct and logical sentences as you can.

I wish	you	were	come.
	I	could	rich.
		would	
		had	

_____

_____

_____

_____

_____

_____

2 (Circle) the correct alternative in the following sentences. Sometimes two are possible.

1 I really wish I *can / could / was able to* speak another language.
2 I wish it *wasn't / wouldn't be / isn't* so cold. I hate the winter.
3 It's time we *have / had / have had* a holiday.
4 Our holiday was a disaster. I'd rather we *didn't go / hadn't gone / weren't going*.
5 The party was brilliant after you left. You should *stay / had stayed / have stayed* longer.
6 I wish you *don't speak / didn't speak / wouldn't speak* so quickly. I can't follow you.
7 What were you doing on that wall? Supposing you *'d fallen / would fall / hadn't fallen*?
8 She'd rather her grandchildren *live / lived / had lived* nearer. Then she could see them more often.

3 Expressions of regret

1 Rewrite the sentences so they have similar meanings. Use the words in brackets.

1 I'm sorry I didn't invite him to the party. (wish)

_____

2 Why weren't you watching the road? (should)

_____

3 I regret saying that to her. (If only)

_____

4 I shouldn't have hit him. (wish)

_____

5 I don't want you to tell her. ('d rather)

_____

6 I don't like it when Meg stays out so late. (wish)

_____

7 I regret I didn't tell him that I loved him. (should)

_____

2 Write sentences to express these people's wishes and regrets. Use the expressions from exercise 1.

1 _____

2 _____

3 _____
_____

4 _____
_____

5 _____
_____

6 _____
_____

4 What I wish I'd known …

Read and complete the article with words from the box.

A letter to my 16-year-old-self

| if   would   hadn't   should   'd |

Dear Marianne,

¹ _____ only I'd enjoyed my school days more and ² _____ wished my childhood away. I ³ _____ have realized how lucky I was to be a child, a time when you have no stress, no bills, no husbands, no babies and no job! I ⁴ _____ have had a lot more fun if I ⁵ _____ just enjoyed the moment.

| should   only   could   couldn't   wouldn't   would |

Dear George,

If ⁶ _____ I had known how precocious I was, I ⁷ _____ have been such a clever clogs! I now realize I must have really annoyed my classmates. I ⁸ _____ have saved up and bought some contact lenses, then I might have looked less nerdy and made more friends. I ⁹ _____ also have been able to see when playing rugby – a distinct advantage. I ¹⁰ _____ have done with putting on a bit of weight, too. I ¹¹ _____ get a girlfriend because I was so skinny.

| if   wouldn't   could   imagine   realized |
| won't   have   unless |

Dear Sue,

If I ¹² _____ give you any advice, first, ignore Simon, the kid who calls you fat. ¹³ _____ I had ¹⁴ _____ at your age what a waste of time it is to listen to bullies, I ¹⁵ _____ have worn oversized clothes for the next four years. Just ¹⁶ _____ how he will look years from now when he's bald, then you ¹⁷ _____ feel so intimidated.
Secondly, say thank you to Mum and Dad *all* the time ¹⁸ _____ they're really nagging you about being out late. I wouldn't ¹⁹ _____ become an actress without their support.
So, 16-year-old me, give them the biggest hug – they deserve it!
Looking back, I wish I could!

Third conditional

5 Regrets

1 Below are the top five regrets in life. Read the article quickly. Which regret goes with which paragraph? Write them in.

> 'I wish I had said what I was really thinking.'   'I wish I hadn't worked so hard!'
> 'I wish I had been true to myself.'   'I wish I had done more!'
> 'I wish we had stayed in touch.'

Top **five** regrets in life

As we progress through our lives, we sometimes pause and ponder on what might have been and how the choices, decisions, and behaviour from our past have affected who we are today. Hindsight gives us a clearer vision of what we should have done, and we can't help but wonder what we would change about our past actions if we could do it all again! Here are our top five regrets.

1 _____

Too often we live our lives trying to please other people rather than fulfilling our own dreams. Many of us wish we had made braver choices, ones that would have allowed us to follow our real passion in life. Many of us believe that if we hadn't always chosen to please other people, we would have very different lives, jobs, or partners today.

2 _____

Many of us who are parents realize as we get older that the treadmill of work has been a barrier to spending enough quality time with our children. We wonder whether it was really necessary to stay so late at work, and we feel sad that we can never claim back their childhood. If we hadn't spent so much time at the office, we might have more happy memories of playing with our kids and reading bedtime stories. Children grow up quickly!

3 _____

Too often we suppress our feelings to keep the peace and are too scared to say what we really feel. As a result, we end up feeling resentful, which drains our energy. In the past, if we had said what we truly believed, we wouldn't now feel bitter and full of regret. It's never too late, though. Be strong and say what you feel (within reason) and you will find you have more positive energy in your life.

4 _____

Established friendships are crucial for our mental well-being. Unfortunately, too many of us lose contact with old friends. One of our top five regrets is the loss of golden friendships that have slipped away over the years because we were too busy. So, although social networking sites like Facebook and Twitter make it easier to stay in touch these days, it takes more than a status update, a quick text, or a tweet to keep a good friendship on track.

Regrets Behind You

2 Complete these third conditional regrets with information from the text. Which regret do they go with?

1 If I hadn't always put my work first, I could have _____ with my children. ☐

2 I would have had more fun in my life if I _____ more risks. ☐

3 I wouldn't feel bitter now if I hadn't _____ to say what I really feel. ☐

4 I'd have many more friends now if I'd _____ with them over the years. ☐

5 If only I hadn't tried to please other people all the time, I would have _____ my own dreams. ☐

5 _____

Many of us do not realize that we could have been happier if we'd moved outside of our comfort zone. Instead, we got stuck in familiar routines and forgot to look around for new opportunities. When we look back at our actions, we often wish we had taken risks and been more fulfilled. Just think, if we hadn't compromised with the safe option, you might have experienced more in your life and had a lot more fun!

3 Rearrange the words to make excuses in the third conditional.

1 wouldn't / been / if / ill / hadn't / shellfish / had / I / I / have / the

2 phoned / had / had / if / you / have / time / would / I / the / I

3 if / known / had / I / the jumper / machine-washable / wasn't / wouldn't / I / bought / have / it

4 if / it / own / my / eyes / seen / with / hadn't / I / wouldn't / believed / I / have / it

4 Complete the second sentence to express the excuse in a different way.

1 I didn't know you had a mobile. I didn't contact you.

   If I'd known you had a mobile, I could/would have contacted you.

2 I didn't send you a postcard because I didn't know your address.

   If I _____
   _____ a postcard.

3 I didn't remember when your birthday was. That's why I didn't buy you a present.

   If _____
   _____ .

4 I broke the speed limit because I was rushing my wife to the hospital.

   If _____
   _____ .

5 I'm sorry I'm late. I forgot to set my alarm clock.

   If _____
   _____ .

All conditionals

6 Revision of all conditionals

Put the verb in brackets in the correct tense to form either the first, second, third, or zero conditional. There are also some examples of mixed conditionals.

1 If I still _____ (feel) sick, I _____ (not go) on holiday next weekend.

2 You make such delicious chocolate cakes! If you _____ (sell) them, you _____ (make) a fortune.

3 Hello, Liz. Are you still looking for Pat? If I _____ (see) her, I _____ (tell) her you want to speak to her.

4 If Alice _____ (go) to Exeter University, she _____ (not met) her husband, Andrew.

5 **A** Does she love him?

   B Of course she does. If she _____ (not love) him, she _____ (not marry) him.

6 If you _____ (buy) two bottles of shampoo, you _____ (get) one free.

7 **A** What _____ you _____ (do) if you _____ (see) a ghost?

   B I _____ (run) away!

8 If we _____ (bring) the map with us, we _____ (not be) lost.

9 You are lucky to be alive. If you _____ (not have) a smoke alarm, the house _____ (burn down) with you in it.

10 You were very rude to Max. If I _____ (be) you, I _____ (apologize).

11 Ashley is allergic to cheese. If he _____ (eat) it, he _____ (get) a rash.

12 We've run out of petrol. If you _____ (listen) to me, you _____ (hear) me saying that we were running low. Then we _____ (not be) stuck here now.

Ways of introducing conditionals

1 Conditionals can be introduced in a variety of ways other than with *if*.

unless

Unless means *except if.*

> We'll go swimming **unless** it rains.

> **Unless** there's a strike, I'll be at work tomorrow.

in case

In case means the first action is a precaution: it happens because the second action *might* happen.

> I'll take my umbrella **in case** it rains.

> Take your boots **in case** it's muddy.

Supposing ... / Suppose ... / Imagine ...

These mean the same as *Imagine if ... ?* or *What if ... ?*

They are questions, and they come at the beginning of a sentence.

> **Supposing** you could go on holiday tomorrow, where would you go?

> **Imagine** you were rich, what would you buy?

2 In more formal styles, *if* can be dropped and the auxiliary verb inverted. This is common with *had, were,* and *should.*

> **Were** they my children, I wouldn't let them watch so much TV. (If they were my children ...)

> **Had I known** that he was a journalist, I would have said nothing. (If I had known ...)

> **Should** the meeting **overrun**, I'll have to cancel my dinner engagement. (If the meeting should overrun ...)

7 Words other than *if*

1 (Circle) the correct word to complete the sentence.

1 *In case / Imagine* there were no more wars – wouldn't that be wonderful?

2 I'm going to take a cushion to the concert, *in case / unless* the seats are hard.

3 We'll miss the beginning of the film *if / unless* you hurry.

4 *Unless / In case* you behave yourself, you can't come to the party with us.

5 *Suppose / Should* you got lost, what would you do?

6 I'll take a book *in case / unless* I'm bored on the journey.

7 *Had / Supposing* I understood the problem, I'd have done something about it.

8 *Should / In case* you fail to pay this bill, court action will be taken.

2 Rewrite these sentences using the words in brackets.

1 I won't come if they don't invite me. (unless)

_____

_____

2 What would you do if he left you? (supposing)

_____

_____

3 If you had learned to play tennis, would you have been a champion by now? (suppose)

_____

_____

4 We're going to install a smoke alarm. There may be a fire. (in case)

_____

_____

5 She won't get that job if she doesn't learn to speak French. (unless)

_____

_____

6 If the lifeguard hadn't been there, what would have happened? (imagine)

_____

_____

7 I won't go out this evening. Justin might ring. (in case)

_____

_____

8 I'll be at my desk until 6.00 if you need to speak to me about the matter. (should)

_____

_____

Vocabulary

8 Similar words, different meaning

These adjective pairs are easy to confuse. Complete the sentences with the correct adjectives.

unreadable   illegible

1 I couldn't work out who the letter was from. The signature was completely _____ .

2 I know Shakespeare is very popular, but I find him totally _____ .

childish   childlike

3 Manisha is so _____ . She's always having temper tantrums.

4 It was wonderful to watch the lambs playing. I got such _____ pleasure from it.

sensible   sensitive

5 Sophie is extremely _____ at the moment. Anything you say upsets her.

6 Fabienne is not a very _____ person. She wore high-heeled shoes for our four-mile walk.

true   truthful

7 I've never known her to tell a lie. She's a very _____ person.

8 I can never watch sad films that are based on a _____ story. They always make me cry.

intolerable   intolerant

9 Susan is so _____ of other people. She never accepts anyone else's opinion, and she always thinks she knows best.

10 I find Marek's behaviour _____ . It's unfair to be so selfish.

economic   economical

11 We're in _____ crisis at the moment. James has lost his job and I don't know how we are going to pay the mortgage.

12 It's much more _____ to drive slowly. You get more kilometres for your money.

Phrasal verbs

9 Nouns from phrasal verbs

1 There are many nouns formed from phrasal verbs. Sometimes the verb comes first, sometimes second.
make-up   downfall   upbringing
drawback   outbreak   takeaway

2 Sometimes the noun is related to the phrasal verb.
*I don't use much **make-up**.*
*She **made up** her face very carefully.* = related
Sometimes they are not related.
*The main **drawback** is the cost.* (drawback = disadvantage)
***Draw back** the curtains and let the sunshine in.* (draw back = open)

Complete these sentences with the nouns in the box.

outcome	breakthrough	outbreak	takeaway
check-up	breakdown	comeback	feedback
outlook	downfall		

1 The _____ of communication between management and workers means the strike will continue.

2 His career has suffered recently, but with a new album and a world tour, he's determined to make a _____ .

3 I go to the dentist twice a year for a _____ .

4 The _____ of the local elections is that the Green party has won 12 new seats.

5 The weather should be fine over the next few days, and the _____ for the weekend is warm and sunny.

6 There has been an _____ of salmonella, infecting 83 people in just over two weeks.

7 There has been a significant _____ in the search to find a cure for breast cancer.

8 Online companies often ask customers for _____ because it is a quick, cheap way of doing market research.

9 We're having an Indian _____ for supper.

10 He used to be a highly successful athlete, but taking too many drugs was his _____ .

Listening

10 Homeless to Harvard

1 🎧 Listen to Clare trying to inspire her son, Harry, to study harder. Match a question in **A** with an answer in **B**.

A	B
1 ☐ When does Harry have his exams?	a Because she had two young children.
2 ☐ Why was it difficult for Clare to study for her degree?	b Because she nags him.
3 ☐ Why does Harry get irritated with his mother?	c On the Internet.
4 ☐ Where did Clare find out about Liz Murray?	d Next month.
5 ☐ What did Liz and her sister sometimes eat for their dinner?	e Toothpaste.
6 ☐ Who does Liz now give speeches with?	f She's an author and speaker.
7 ☐ How old was Liz when her mother died?	g 15.
8 ☐ What did Liz's mother always believe?	h Bill Clinton.
9 ☐ How did Liz afford to go to Harvard?	i One day life is going to get better.
10 ☐ What does Liz do now?	j She got a scholarship from *The New York Times*.

2 🎧 Listen again. Match the lines to make sentences.

1	If Harry does more revision,	a	she would have got her degree sooner.
2	If Clare had worked harder at school,	b	she wouldn't have died so young.
3	If Liz's mother hadn't been a drug addict,	c	he might do better in his exams.
4	If Liz hadn't gone to night classes,	d	she wouldn't have completed her high school education.
5	If Liz's teacher hadn't taken her to Harvard,	e	he might regret it one day.
6	If Harry spends all his time on the PlayStation,	f	she may never have considered studying there.

3 🎧 Listen again. Who says these things, Clare (**C**) or Harry (**H**)?

1 I wasted so many years just watching TV. ☐
2 Give me a break. ☐
3 You just don't realize how lucky you are. ☐
4 ... and you think I'm bad. ☐
5 That is desperate. ☐
6 ... she never forgot her mother's mantra ☐
7 You've made your point. ☐

4 Look at the tapescript on p86 and check your answers.

Pronunciation

11 Ways of pronouncing *ea*

1 There are several different ways of pronouncing the letters *ea*. Look at the examples in the columns below.

/e/	/iː/	/ɪə/
bread	meat	fear

/eə/	/eɪ/	/ɜː/
wear	break	learn

2 🎧 Put these words into the correct column according to the pronunciation of *ea*.

dear	thread	pearl	leap
tear (n)	bear	pear	leapt
tear (v)	cheat	heal	meant
scream	clear	health	reason
steak	deaf	great	search
breath	death	gear	swear
breathe	earth	jealous	theatre
breadth	beast	lead (v)	weary
hear	beard	lead (n)	weapon

12

Articles • Determiners • Demonstratives
• Nouns in groups • *be* and *have* • Emphasis in speaking

Time flies

Articles

1 *a, the,* or zero article?

1 Complete the sentences with *a, the,* or nothing (zero article).

1 Excuse me! Is there _____ bank near here?

2 **A** I haven't got any money.

  B I'm going to _____ bank. I'll get you some.

3 Has _____ postman been this morning?

4 My brother works as _____ postman.

5 We've seen a house we want to move to. It's got _____ views over fields, and there's _____ lovely garden at _____ back.

6 **A** Where's Nick?

  B In _____ garden.

7 I bought _____ dog to protect myself against _____ burglars.

8 Tony joined _____ Police Dog Unit because he likes working with _____ dogs.

9 We went out for _____ meal last night. _____ food was excellent. I don't usually like _____ Chinese food, but _____ duck was superb.

2 Complete the newspaper article with *a, an, the,* or nothing.

It's **never** too early

Abha, 7, gains her GCSE in computing

[1] _____ girl aged seven went into *The Guinness Book of Records* yesterday when she became [2] _____ youngest pupil ever to pass [3] _____ national exam.

Abha Subramanian, from Manchester, studied at [4] _____ Ellesmere College near her home several evenings [5] _____ week, finally gaining [6] _____ grade C in [7] _____ computer studies and earning a place in [8] _____ record books.

She says: 'I think [9] _____ computers are easy but [10] _____ exam was quite hard.' She praised her teacher, James Nolan, [11] _____ founder and principal of [12] _____ college. 'He's [13] _____ nice teacher – he tells us [14] _____ jokes!'

Dr Nolan commented: 'You must have [15] _____ faith in children. They can make [16] _____ paper planes one minute and write [17] _____ computer program [18] _____ next. [19] _____ pupils at my school aren't prodigies – they are just interested and motivated. They are [20] _____ example of what [21] _____ rest of [22] _____ country could be doing.

It is Dr Nolan's firm belief that age 18 is already too old for [23] _____ university and [24] _____ academic world. He maintains that students of this age have passed their mental peak.

Determiners

2 all and every

1 (Circle) the correct answer.

1 Anna is such a show-off, she thinks she knows *all / everything*.

2 My driving test was a complete disaster. *All / Everything* went wrong.

3 Kate didn't say where she was going. *All / Everything* she said was that she was going out.

4 *All / Every* child in the class failed the exam.

5 *All / Everything* I want for my birthday is to lie in bed until midday.

6 I'm starving. *All / Everything* I've eaten today is a packet of crisps.

7 I really don't get on with my new boss. I disagree with *all / everything* she says.

8 I can't go higher than £500 for the car. That's *everything / all* I can afford.

9 Megan couldn't believe her luck. *All / Every* topic she had revised the night before came up in the exam.

10 The film was so boring that *all / everybody* fell asleep.

2 (Circle) the correct answer.

1 I have three dogs. *All / Every* of them love going for a walk, but *neither / none* of them likes being brushed.

2 You can borrow *either / each* the Renault or the Volvo. They're *all / both* in the garage.

3 My two daughters are *each / both* good at languages, but *none / neither* of them can do maths at all.

4 I have a shower *every / each* day.

5 I have *any / no* idea how I spend all my money. At the end of *every / either* month, it's all gone.

6 I know *every / each* word of his songs by heart.

7 There are 15 rooms in this hotel. *Each / Every* room is a little different.

8 You can have *either / each* an orange or an apple, but you can't have *either / both*.

9 **A** Tea or coffee?
   B *Either / Neither*, thanks. I've got to rush.

10 **A** Red wine or white?
   B *Either / Neither*, whichever is open.

11 I know *either / both* Robert and his brother, but I don't like *both / either* of them.

12 I have four brothers. *Every / Each* of us is different.

Demonstratives

3 this, that, these, those

Put *this*, *that*, *these*, or *those* into each gap.

1 _____ shoes are killing me. I can't wait to take them off.

2 (On the phone) Hello. _____ is Beth. Can I speak to Kate?

3 _____ was a wonderful film, wasn't it?

4 I knew Jenny at university. In _____ days, she had long blonde hair.

5 **A** Anything else?
   B No, _____ 's all for today, thanks.

6 Well, _____ 'll be £5.50, please.

7 I can't get _____ ring off my finger. It's stuck.

8 You just can't get proper sausages _____ days.

9 Come here and tidy up _____ mess right now!

10 Listen to _____ . It says in the paper that life's been found on Mars.

11 Did you ever hear from _____ girl you met on holiday last year?

12 I was in the pub last night when _____ bloke came up to me and hit me.

13 **A** I got a parking fine today.
   B _____ 'll teach you a lesson.

14 Who were _____ people you were talking to last night?

15 What was _____ noise? Didn't you hear it?

Revision of articles, determiners, and demonstratives

4 Searching for Sugar Man

Complete the article about the documentary *Searching for Sugar Man* with the words in the boxes. Each word can only be used once only.

Searching for Sugar Man

RODRIGUEZ – one of the greatest 70s rock icons – but it took the world over 40 years to discover him!

| a couple of | the (x 2) | his | little |
| a great deal of | this | several | enough |

Rodriguez was first discovered in Detroit, Michigan, in ¹ _____ late 60s by ² _____ well-known music producers who were struck by ³ _____ touching music and expressive lyrics. There was ⁴ _____ anticipation when he recorded his first album, *Cold Fact*, in 1970. It included his best-known song, 'Sugar Man'. ⁵ _____ song earned ⁶ _____ good reviews and Rodriguez was compared to Bob Dylan. Unfortunately, this wasn't ⁷ _____ of a recommendation to ensure its success, and ⁸ _____ album bombed in the US. A second album, *Coming from Reality*, also had ⁹ _____ success in the US, and Rodriguez disappeared into obscurity.

| every | no | the | a | many of | both | this |

However, unbeknown to him, Rodriguez' two albums had arrived in South Africa where ¹⁰ _____ of them had become hugely popular in the 1970s. ¹¹ _____ success was mainly because the powerful music and lyrics reflected so well the message of the anti-apartheid movement of the time. Despite there being ¹² _____ promotion at all on ¹³ _____ radio, word of the albums spread, and over half a million records were sold. Nearly ¹⁴ _____ student in South Africa owned ¹⁵ _____ copy of *Cold Fact*. Rodriguez' music influenced a generation of fans, just as Jimi Hendrix's songs had become important to ¹⁶ _____ the US troops in Vietnam.

| the | some | more | anything |
| nobody | a wealth of | his |

Over the next two decades, his popularity grew. Rodriguez had ¹⁷ _____ fans than Elvis Presley and the Beatles, but ¹⁸ _____ knew who he was or ¹⁹ _____ else about him. There were even ²⁰ _____ rumours that he had taken ²¹ _____ own life whilst on stage! This was, of course, before the advent of ²² _____ Internet. Today, a search on Google would have quickly uncovered ²³ _____ information.

| the | a | an | one | most | these | all |

The riddle of Rodriguez is what the documentary film *Searching for Sugar Man* sets out to solve. After years of searching, Swedish director Malek Bendjelloul finally discovered the singer-songwriter alive and well, and still living in Detroit, where he worked as ²⁴ _____ builder and had brought up three daughters. It was ²⁵ _____ of ²⁶ _____ daughters who filled in ²⁷ _____ of the blanks about his life.

There is now ²⁸ _____ official Sugar Man website. His albums have been re-released and are available to his fans ²⁹ _____ over the world, and *Searching for Sugar Man* won Best Documentary in ³⁰ _____ 2013 Oscars.

Nouns in groups

1 There are three main ways that we can put nouns together.

noun + noun   noun + 's + noun

post office   *my wife's sister*

headache   *the doctor's surgery*

face-lift   *the dog's bowl*

noun + preposition + noun

the end of the garden

a story about compassion

the arrival of the police

2 Sometimes more than one structure can be used.

the Prime Minister's arrival

the arrival of the Prime Minister

the floor of the living room

the living room floor

the car door handle

the handle on the car door

But usually only one pattern is possible.

the back of the car

NOT ~~the car back~~   ~~the car's back~~

3 Sometimes there is a change in meaning.

the cat's food = the food that belongs to one particular cat

*The dog has eaten the **cat's food**.*

cat food = food for cats in general

*Can you buy some more **cat food** when you go out?*

IT'S A NEW FLAVOR, HENRY, HE WANTS YOU TO TRY IT FIRST.

4 We use the noun + noun pattern (compound nouns) for everyday established combinations.

a love film, a horror film

For less established combinations, we prefer noun + preposition + noun.

a film about horses

NOT ~~a horse film~~

5 Combining nouns

Combine the words in brackets using one of the three patterns. Sometimes there is more than one answer.

1 Your coat's on the _____ (back, chair).

2 You've just spilt the _____ (milk, cat).

3 Can you buy some _____ (paper, toilet)? We've run out.

4 I never listened to my _____ (advice, parents).

5 Can you buy a _____ (wine, bottle) to have with dinner?

6 What did that _____ (road, sign) say? Did you see it?

7 It's such a mess in here. There are empty _____ (wine, bottles) everywhere.

8 The _____ (Prime Minister, duties) include entertaining heads of state.

9 The _____ (my shoe, heel) has come off.

10 Can I borrow your _____ (brush, hair)?

11 What happened at the _____ (film, end)?

12 Here is _____ (today, news).

13 Where is the nearest _____ (Underground, station)?

14 It's my _____ (anniversary, parents, wedding) next week.

15 The _____ (company, success) is due to its efficiency.

16 I've got a _____ (fortnight, holiday) next month.

17 The _____ (government, economic policy) is confusing.

18 The annual _____ (rate, inflation) is about 4%.

19 Are there any _____ (coffee, cups) in your bedroom? There are none in the kitchen.

20 Do you want a _____ (coffee, cup)?

Vocabulary

6 Hot verbs – *be, have*

1 Match the words and expressions with *be* or *have*. Tick (✔) the correct column.

be	have	
✔		fed up with sb/sth
	✔	the right to do sth
		the nerve to do sth
		on the safe side
		in touch with sb
		a word with sb
		no point in doing sth
		on one's mind
		up to date
		no chance of doing sth

2 Complete the sentences with one of the expressions from exercise 1 in the correct form.

1 My job is so boring. **I'm really fed up with** it.

2 If you don't like your meal, you _____ complain to the manager.

3 Thank you for your interview, Miss Clarke. We _____ you as soon as we've made a decision about the job.

4 I can't stop thinking about my ex-girlfriend. She _____ always _____ .

5 Mrs Bennett! Can I _____ you for a minute? It's about your son Ben.

6 Jack was so cheeky! He _____ tell me that this dress didn't suit me!

7 I've got extra holiday insurance just in case. I always like _____ .

8 Well, I'll apply for the manager's job, but I know I _____ getting it.

9 Wait here. If you don't like heights, there _____ climbing up the tower with us.

10 In my job, it is important to _____ with what's going on in the financial market.

Prepositions revision

7 Noun + preposition

Complete the sentences with a preposition or a combination of prepositions.

1 After running up the stairs, I was _____ breath.

2 You make some silly mistakes, but _____ general, your work has been good.

3 I went on holiday _____ my own, because sometimes I like to be _____ myself.

4 I got a cheque _____ £500 in the post.

5 There has been a rise _____ the number of violent crimes.

6 The difference _____ you and me is that I don't mind hard work.

7 I can think of no reason _____ her strange behaviour.

8 It took a long time to find a solution _____ the problem.

9 I need some information _____ global warming.

10 I'm having trouble _____ my car. It won't start in the mornings.

11 In the accident, there was quite a bit of damage _____ my car.

12 Investigators are trying to find the cause _____ the accident.

13 I've got to do my homework _____ tomorrow.

14 I don't see James any more. I haven't been _____ touch with him for years.

15 Did you get an invitation _____ David's wedding?

Listening

8 You're never too old

1 🎧 Listen to Mary Hobson talking about her life. Mark the statements true (✓) or false (✗).

1. ☐ She wrote a book before she was 40.
2. ☐ She took care of her sick husband.
3. ☐ She didn't read all of *War and Peace*.
4. ☐ She learnt Russian from an old lady.
5. ☐ The happiest time of her life was in the 1960s.
6. ☐ Recently, she's started to lose her memory.
7. ☐ She loves Moscow but isn't crazy about the cold weather.
8. ☐ She plans to continue learning Greek.

2 🎧 Listen again and complete these lines with the exact words from the text.

1. I am what _____ a late developer.
2. We were _____ , we lived on national assistance.
3. _____ was his fault, of course.
4. Then it _____ : I hadn't read it at all, I'd only read a translation,
5. _____ the town _____ the country any day.
6. I won't be able to _____ forever.
7. When I can't _____ my front steps, I'll perfect my Greek.
8. _____ I have my books, I'll be happy.

3 There is one mistake in each of these sentences. Find it and correct it.

1. Mary was 62 when she went to a university.
2. Her husband was talented jazz musician.
3. She believes that you've only got a life so you mustn't waste it.
4. Mary decided to learn the Russian and Greek.
5. She read the all of *War and Peace* in Russian.
6. She prefers the town over a countryside.
7. She loves lying in the bed listening to the snow.
8. He lost the speech and the use of the right side of his body.

Pronunciation

9 Nouns and verbs

In the chart the nouns end in an unvoiced sound (/s/, /f/, /θ/), and the verbs end in a voiced sound (/z/, /v/, /ð/).

🎧 Complete the chart with the words and the phonetics. The vowel sound or the spelling changes.

Noun		Verb	
advice			/ədvaɪz/
		to use	
abuse			
	/bɪliːf/		
			/rɪliːv/
grief			
	/ɪkskjuːs/		
breath			
		to halve	
	/haʊs/		
safe			
			/beɪð/

10 Emphasis in speaking

🎧 Mark where the main stress is in **B**'s replies. Listen, check, and repeat.

1. **A** Why didn't you do your homework last night?
   B I <u>did</u> do it.
2. **A** Who made this mark on the carpet?
   B I did it. Sorry.
3. **A** Did you know that Johann and Maria are coming tonight?
   B I knew Johann was coming.
4. **A** Did you know that Johann and Maria are coming tonight?
   B I knew that ages ago.
5. **A** Who told Gran that I crashed her car?
   B I didn't tell her.
6. **A** I wish you hadn't told Gran I crashed her car.
   B I didn't tell her.
7. **A** I lost all my money playing cards.
   B I told you.
8. **A** You don't like Mike and Annie, do you?
   B I like Annie.
9. **A** Why don't you like Annie?
   B I do like Annie. I think she's great.
10. **A** I feel so sorry for Annie. Nobody likes her.
    B I like her.

Tapescripts

UNIT 1

Exercise 11, parts 1 and 2

Missing home

N = Nancy   A = Amy

N Hi, Amy! Phew … Just finished my first assignment – I hope it's okay. Fancy tea and cake in my room to celebrate? It's one of my mum's homemade chocolate cakes. She brought it with her when she came to visit last weekend.

A Sure! Always got time for cake. I haven't had any home-cooked food for ages. I've been living off chips from the college canteen!

N Eugh! Those chips are so greasy! I really miss home-cooked food – my dad's chicken curry, and my mum's apple pie. I can't be bothered to cook for myself.

A Know what you mean. It's too much effort to cook for one. Mmm! This cake is great! Tastes yummy. I was so looking forward to university, but now I'm here I feel homesick.

N You, too? Thought it was just me. Everyone else seems to be having such a good time, but I feel quite lonely.

A I know how you feel. I'm missing all my friends from home. It takes time to get to know people.

N My flatmates are out partying most nights. I've always been quite happy staying in, having friends round, and watching TV.

A Me, too! Can't really do that here as our rooms are so small. I miss having a whole house to walk around in. And have you seen the state of the communal kitchen? It's gross!

N Yes. Students aren't the tidiest. I suppose we're not used to looking after ourselves.

A I must admit, I do like the independence – no one asking what time you'll be home.

N And we also get to eat as much chocolate cake as we want! Want some more?

UNIT 2

Exercise 7, parts 1, 2 and 3

Off the beaten track

P = Presenter   KM = Kay Morris   VS = Vicky Smith   GB = Gary

P Welcome to *Off the Beaten Track*. Today I am joined by Kay Morris, a tour operator, Vicky Smith, a travel writer, and Gary Braithwaite, a film director who has filmed in some breathtaking locations. Good morning, everyone!

KM, VS, GB Good morning!

P Now, Kay, you're here to tell us about your most recent excursion.

KM Yes, I'm always looking for adventurous holiday experiences for my clients, so I was thrilled when I was invited to stay in an eco-lodge in the Ecuadorian Amazon, owned and run by the legendary Huaorani Tribe. I've been travelling for over 30 years, but meeting the Huaorani people was a totally new experience. Nothing could have prepared me for the enthusiastic welcome we received – truly amazing. We spent our days on silent rivers in dugout canoes fishing, and learning tricks of survival in the rainforest. In the evenings, we sat with the villagers around a crackling fire eating the food we'd caught and exchanging stories about our different lives. This is the perfect destination for people who are looking for a completely different holiday.

P Thank you, Kay! Now my next guest is Vicky Smith, a travel writer who has written a series of books for the more adventurous tourist. Her latest book focuses on places to stay, and as she discovered, there are interesting alternatives to five-star hotels! Could you tell us, Vicky, about one place that stands out for you?

VS There are so many enchanting places to stay in around the world. However, the most memorable for me was a bed and breakfast in Vienna. At first, I was staying in a five-star hotel – it was supposedly a romantic haunt for spies and celebrities – but for £250 a night, it had the atmosphere of an airport lounge and not a James Bond lookalike to be seen! So, I gathered my luggage and went to 'The Rooms', a family run B and B in the centre of Vienna. I was shown into a comfortable room with a sunlit terrace and stunning views of the city, its cathedrals, and church towers. For only £60 a night, I had a great breakfast, the cleanest facilities, and the friendliest atmosphere I've ever experienced in all my travels. It really does pay to look around for alternative accommodation.

P Well, thank you, Vicky! And our final guest today is Gary Braithwaite, a film director from New Zealand. You spend a lot of time, Gary, searching for the right locations to add authenticity to your films. Why is this?

GB The location is just so crucial to the atmosphere of the movie. And having grown up in the middle of nowhere in a small town in New Zealand, I've always craved adventure. I needed a real American experience to inspire me for my latest film, so I decided to visit the largest Native American reservation in the US, the Navajo Nation, which extends across the boundaries of Arizona, Utah, and New Mexico. It's like a separate country; it has its own flag, time zone, and language. It was here that I found the America I had imagined from thousands of miles away in New Zealand. I powwowed with the other men, rode horses bareback, and rounded up cattle. This experience really influenced my movie. Forget Disneyland! If you want a true American adventure, visit the Navajo Nation.

P How interesting! Thank you, and thank you to all my guests! I hope you'll tune in again next week.

UNIT 3

Exercise 9, parts 1 and 2

It's complicated!

J = Julie   A = Amy

J Hi, Amy! Did you have a good weekend?

A Yes, thanks, Julie! Taylor and I just lazed about all Sunday afternoon reading the papers. Actually, I read a really interesting article in *The Sunday Times* – it reminded me of Linda and Graham.

J Did it? Why was that?

A Well, it was all about how the hatred between divorced couples can sometimes, over time, develop into love again.

J Really?

A Yeah! You know, like in that film a few years back. What was it called? It had Meryl Streep and Alec Baldwin in it. It was about a divorced couple who got back together.

J Oh, yes, I think it was called 'It's complicated'. Steve Martin was in it, too. It was really funny.

A Yes, that was it – 'It's Complicated'. Well, you know how in the film Alec Baldwin starts yearning for his old life with his ex-wife, Meryl Streep. You know, because she shares his memories and she's the mother of his children, and she knows how to cook his favourite food and ...

J Yeah, and the novelty of his new, young wife has worn off and ...

A Yes! And he's exhausted trying to keep up with her!

J Anyway, this article was saying how many divorced couples can become best friends again because they have their memories and so many things in common.

J Actually, I can believe that. So, what about Linda and Graham? They've been divorced for ages.

A Exactly!

J Surely they're not back together? They couldn't stand each other!

A Well, you really won't believe this! They met again at Linda's grandma's funeral last week. Graham and the grandma had always got along really well. Anyhow, they started reminiscing, and all the animosity just slipped away.

J Ah! That's lovely.

A I think they realized how much they had in common, and that perhaps they'd not worked hard enough at their marriage, and they've started dating again.

J They haven't! That's amazing! I hope it works out for them.

A Yes, me too! I really like them both.

J You know, I think we sometimes give up on things too easily. You have to work hard at relationships.

A That's very true! Fingers crossed about Linda and Graham. It would be such a happy ending.

UNIT 4

Exercise 8, part 1

Not the whole truth!

1

Lauren Hi, Susie! Do you like my dress? I bought it especially for the party. It cost an absolute fortune.

Susie It really suits you, and it's a lovely colour. It really hugs your figure.

2

David Happy Birthday, Alan! How old are you now?

Alan Forty-two! Can you believe it?

David No way! You don't look a day over 25!

3

Officer Do you know you were driving at 100 mph?

Charlie Sorry, officer! I had no idea how fast I was going.

4

Wife How come you're home so late? Where have you been? I told you I would have dinner ready for seven o'clock!

Husband Honey, I'm so sorry! I had a meeting with my boss and it finished late.

5

Tom Wow ... saucepans ... thanks, Mum. What a useful birthday present!

Mum Well, I thought that now you've moved in to your own flat, you can start cooking for your friends and for me when I visit!

Tom A brilliant present, Mum! Just what I've always wanted!

6

Fiona Isn't he the cutest? They say you always think your own baby is beautiful, but in this case he really is.

Beth You must be so proud. He's adorable ... looks just like his dad.

7

Pat Could we have the bill, please?

Waiter Of course, Madam! I'll just get it for you.

Peter Oh no! I don't believe it! I'll have to pay next time. I seem to have come out without my wallet.

8

Alistair I hope you like the chicken vindaloo. I've never cooked it before, and thought it might be too hot.

Colin It's delicious. Nice and spicy. I won't have any more, thank you. I'm rather full.

UNIT 5

Exercise 4, parts 1 and 2

Future Continuous or Future Perfect?

J = Jack   T = Tommy   M = Millie

J Do you ever wonder what you'll be doing in ten years' time?

T Yeah! I think about it all the time. I'll be 25, and I'll be Captain Tommy Devoy, and I'll be flying A380s for British Airways.

J Says you! How can you be so sure?

T Oh, I can see it now – I'll be based at Heathrow, and I'll be living in London, flying to far-off countries like Singapore, Hong Kong, Brazil and ...

J Huh! You'd better fly to New York, too, Tommy, because that's where I'll be living. I'll be in a deluxe apartment on Fifth Avenue, in the heart of Manhattan.

T So, what will you be doing in New York?

J I'm going to be a lawyer for one of the best law firms in New York City.

T Ugh! Law's boring.

M Well, I don't understand you two at all. What's so great about living in a big city? It's just millions of people rushing around. By the time I'm 30, I'll be living somewhere really beautiful and peaceful in the north of England, like the Lake District, and by then, I'll have saved enough money to buy a lovely, big, old farmhouse, and I'll have lots of animals.

J It sounds grim to me. I'd go mad living in the country. Give me the city life any time. While you're chatting to sheep and pigs, I'll be partying with celebrities.

T Yeah, I'm with Jack on this. And, anyway, Millie, how come you'll have enough money to buy a farmhouse?

M From my swimming, of course! I'm aiming to swim for Great Britain at the next Olympics, and I'll be an Olympic medallist. And, after I've become famous, I'll design my own brand of swimwear and make enough money to buy my farmhouse.

T To be an Olympic medallist, you'll have to give up on the rest of life and train from morning 'til night.

M Yeah, I know. That's OK by me.

J But I'll be going to the coolest clubs in New York. And by the time I'm 30, I'll have married a rich film star who will love city life as much as me, and we'll be living in a huge, swanky apartment overlooking Central Park.

M Well, that's not my kind of life.

T And by the time I'm 30, I'll be living in a penthouse flat in London overlooking the River Thames with a gorgeous girlfriend who earns a fortune in the city.

M Huh! In your dreams, Tommy! You'll be lucky to get a girlfriend at all by the time you're 30, let alone a rich, pretty one.

T Hey, watch it, Millie! The girls will be queuing up for me. You'll see!

UNIT 6

Exercise 11, parts 1 and 2

A job interview

I = interviewer   J = Jane

I Good morning, Jane! Please take a seat.

J Thank you!

I Did it take you long to get here today?

J No, I live near Bristol so it was less than thirty minutes, and there was very little traffic.

I Good! So, tell me a bit about yourself, and what you can offer Perfect Petfood Ltd.

J Well, I've always loved animals. I had a horse when I was a girl, and we always had lots of dogs and cats at home. I knew from a young age I wanted to work with animals. I also have excellent people skills and a confident personality, which makes me an ideal candidate to promote your high quality pet food products. I am passionate about providing the best for animals.

I Do you know much about our company?

J Well, I have looked on your website and see that you believe in providing only the best quality products for animals, and you are one of the few pet food companies that have organic food for dogs and cats. The organic range is a market bestseller endorsed by several high-profile celebrity pet owners.

I You seem to know a great deal about our company. Could you give me some more information on your key skills and strengths? How is your previous experience relevant to this position?

J Well, I know it's a different field, but I was top sales person for the beauty department at Selfridges, London. In your job description, you ask for someone who shows initiative, is resourceful, and self-confident. In my previous role, I was able to work on my own without any guidance. I'm brilliant at devising new approaches to make people do what I want them to.

I Well, you seem to have plenty of strengths, Jane. But what about your weaknesses?

J I like to make things happen. I get frustrated if too long is spent sitting around discussing issues without action. I used to feel anxious about giving presentations to lots of people, but I've worked hard at it, and I've been on a couple of courses which have made a huge difference.

I You certainly present yourself very well today, Jane. Why are you leaving your current job?

J Well, as I mentioned earlier, I'm just mad about animals. Working at Selfridges is very glamorous, but my heart isn't in it. I know I'm good at sales, and I want a job that combines my selling skills and love of animals. Think how good I'll be at selling something I'm passionate about!

I Where do you see yourself in five years' time?

J I would hope to be Perfect Petfood's most successful sales manager, inspiring a team of people to make this company an even greater success.

I Thanks! Do you have any questions for me?

UNIT 7

Exercise 9, parts 1 and 2

Not getting on

A = Anya   S = Sophie

A What's wrong, Sophie?

S Oh, nothing much, Anya.

A What do you mean? You look absolutely terrible!

S Oh, I'm just a bit upset, that's all.

A What about? It's not Charlie again, is it?

S Well, yes. He made one or two hurtful remarks this evening.

A One or two? He's always criticizing you these days! I don't know how you can stand it!

S Well, he's been having a bit of trouble at work recently, so he's quite stressed.

A Quite stressed? That's no excuse for being rude to his girlfriend, I don't think. I think his behaviour is totally out of order.

S Yeah, it's getting me down a bit, I must say.

A Well, you really mustn't put up with it any longer, Sophie. You should tell him that if he can't be nicer to you, you won't go out with him anymore.

S Oh, I suppose so. But the trouble is, I'm really crazy about him, you know.

A Well, that's obvious, or you wouldn't put up with all his terrible behaviour.

S And he loves me, too. I know it.

A Well, he's got a funny way of showing it, I must say.

S I suppose you're right. Our relationship hasn't been great lately. We haven't been getting on very well.

A You're not kidding. You've both been completely miserable. Honestly, Sophie, you must do something about it. It's no good waiting until things get magically better. It isn't going to happen.

S OK, OK, Anya! I'll talk to him tonight, I promise.

A Good! Now, put a smile on your face, and let's go and dance!

S All right, all right, just let me go and wash my face first. Can't go on the dance floor looking like this!

A Well, that's true. You could look a bit better than you do!

S Charming, I must say.

A That's more like it! You sound loads better already. Come on, let's go!

UNIT 9

Exercise 11, parts 1 and 2

A small disagreement

M = Megan   H = Harry

M What are you watching?

H Shh!

M It's Saturday night and I can't believe you're watching a bunch of untalented singers all trying desperately to be a famous pop star.

H Shh! Sit down and be quiet! I can't hear the judges' comments.

M Well, if you want my opinion, it's contrived, over the top, and utterly predictable.

H You've changed your tune! When we were at university, this used to be your favourite show. We'd always watch it before we went out on a Saturday night, beers in hand, and giggling over the performances.

M Well, it was compulsive viewing then – it was a new type of reality show. The problem now is that it's the same cheesy format, the same tear-jerking stories to get the audience to feel sorry for them so they'll pick up the phone and vote. The whole thing's a joke!

H Well, I don't agree that it's a joke. There are lots of really talented singers on the show. What about that girl, Ella? She has a fabulous voice. And don't forget that boy band who won last year! They've had two number one hits!

M OK, OK, occasionally there's someone with a good voice. The point I'm trying to make is that most of them can't sing! That boy band only had those big hits because millions of teenage girls think they look cute. If you ask me, you're better off watching a good film rather than being manipulated by TV producers.

H To tell you the truth, I don't mind being manipulated. I'm not stupid. I know what you say is true, but I don't care. There's something enjoyable and addictive about the whole programme. The main point is not to take it too seriously, which you obviously do.

M What worries me is that you just haven't grown up yet. You still think of yourself as a student. I'm going to watch a film in the other room.

H Oh come on, Megan, just chill! Why don't you sit here on the sofa with me, and let's give the contestants a score out of ten, like we did in the old days at uni. I'll make some popcorn, too. It'll be fun.

M Oh, OK then! I suppose it was fun. Go on then! Move over!

UNIT 11

Homeless to Harvard

C = Clare   H = Harry

C I can't believe you're playing on the PlayStation when you have exams next month. I wish something would make you realize how important it is to work hard! I always wish I'd worked harder at school. I wasted so many years just watching TV!

H There you go! And you did OK.

C Eventually! But it took a long time to get my English degree, and I had to study when you and your brother were little. It would have been much easier if I'd just worked harder when I was your age.

H Mum, you're so predictable. You always say the same things. Give me a break!

C You just don't realize how lucky you are. I was reading on the Internet about this girl called Liz Murray; she went from sleeping on the streets to graduating from Harvard.

H Blimey! That's incredible! That is some journey. See, there's hope for me then! What happened to her?

C She grew up in one of the roughest parts of New York, and both her parents were drug addicts. And you think I'm bad because I nag you too much! She now speaks alongside people like Bill Clinton. I bet she would never have believed it when she was eating toothpaste with her sister because they were so hungry.

H Toothpaste! That is desperate. I can't imagine being so hungry that I'd want to eat toothpaste. They were poor. But mum, give it a rest, I'm only 15.

C Well, she was only 15 when her mum died, and then her dad couldn't pay the rent, so she had to sleep on the subway. But she never forgot her mother's mantra, 'one day life is going to get better', and she realized that if she didn't do something now, her life would never get better.

H Hmm! It didn't get better for her mum! So, what did she do? I mean, she was only 15 – she must have been pretty scared sleeping on the subway.

C She took herself to night classes to complete her high school education and did a year's work in a term whilst sleeping rough. Imagine that, Harry!

H Hmm! That is tough. It's hard enough to do school work anyway, let alone when you're homeless. So, how did she get her lucky break?

C Her teacher saw how determined she was and took her to visit Harvard. She decided there and then that she was going to go there. Through sheer hard work, she managed to get a scholarship from *The New York Times*, and now she's a successful author and speaker.

H Yeah, she does make me look a bit pathetic. Hey, but I did get 79% in my Maths test last week.

C Yes. So just think what you could achieve if you put your mind to it. Come on, Harry! When you're a grown man, you will never wish you'd spent more time playing on the PlayStation, but you might regret wasting so much time playing on it.

H OK, Mum! You've made your point. I'll go do some homework. There, PlayStation off, books open. Happy?

C Delirious! Remember, I don't nag you for my benefit. You'll kick yourself one day if you don't work hard now.

UNIT 12

You're never too old

N = Narrator   M = Mary

N Mary Hobson is in her 80s, and nowhere near retirement. She gained a degree in Russian in her 60s, and a PhD at 74. She started learning ancient Greek at 77.

M I am what you might call a 'late developer'. I was 40 before I wrote my first novel, 62 when I went to university. My husband, Neil, was a talented jazz musician, but at 25 he developed a cerebral abscess, losing his speech, and the use of the right side of his body. We were so broke, we lived on national assistance for ages and did everything that was free.

I wrote my first novel while Neil had his weekly music therapy. That 50-minute session was all I had. I used to sit in the ABC cafe in Earls Court and write. Neil was terribly difficult. None of it was his fault, of course, but after 28 years, I thought: 'It's not my fault, either.' I left.

Having snatched a bit of life back, I had to do something with it. My daughter Emma gave me *War and Peace*, and I loved it so much. Then it hit me: I hadn't read it at all, I'd only read a translation, and I so longed to read the actual words. A marvellous, elderly Russian lady taught me the basics, and I enrolled on the Russian-language degree course at the University of London. People talk about 'the time of their lives'. Well, that was mine. Don't let anyone tell you your memory goes with age. Oh, the joy of learning!

I write poetry on buses and trains. I love London. Give me the town over the country any day. I try to go to Moscow every year in the coldest weather. My Russian friends think I'm mad; it hits minus 40, and they find it hellish. I adore lying in bed listening to snow being scraped from the pavements.

I have an overpowering feeling that I don't want to waste any time. I'm sure it's to do with atheism and acceptance of death. I am a dedicated atheist. I regard religion as complete lunacy. You've got one opportunity to be alive: for goodness' sake, don't waste it waiting for an afterlife. There's so much out there.

I won't be able to get out and about forever, so when I can't stagger down my front steps, I'll perfect my Greek. As long as I have my books, I'll be happy.

Answer key

Unit 1

1 1 2 'm … walking
   3 've been walking
   4 was taken
   5 'll take
   6 had taken
   7 've had
   8 were having
   9 'll be having
   10 are … made
   11 has been made
   12 'll have made
   13 're being washed
   14 had been washed
   15 had been washing
   16 sells
   17 will be sold
   19 'll have been teaching
   20 were being taught

2

Active	Simple	Continuous
Present	sells	am walking
Past	walked	were having
Future	will take	will be having
Present Perfect	have had	have been walking
Past Perfect	had taken	had been washing
Future Perfect	will have made	will have been teaching

Passive	Simple	Continuous
Present	are made	are being washed
Past	was taken	were being taught
Future	will be sold	
Present Perfect	has been made	
Past Perfect	had been washed	
Future Perfect	will have been sold	

2 2 It's **been** really cold …
   3 Manchester United **are playing** really well …
   4 I've heard **you have passed** all your exams. Congratulations!
   5 … when my friend **called**.
   6 When I was a little girl, **I always spent** my pocket money on sweets.
   7 **I've been going out** with Paulo for two years …
   8 … Perhaps **I'll get** him a new shirt.
   9 A one-day strike has **been** called by …
   10 … Megan had been working hard and **deserved** to pass all her exams.

3 1 'm looking
   2 don't understand
   3 've … learned
   4 'll call
   5 've been doing
   6 haven't seen
   7 emailed
   8 is studying
   9 'll be accepted
   10 has been chosen
   11 's getting
   12 'll shout
   13 went
   14 stayed
   15 're saving
   16 hadn't realized/didn't realize
   17 have … been doing/were … doing
   18 didn't hear
   19 will be
   20 'll look forward

4 1 1 Our house was built in the 17th century.
   2 My flat's being decorated at the moment.
   3 Has the coffee machine been fixed yet?
   4 While the new kitchen was being built, we ate in restaurants.
   5 When we went up to our hotel room, we found that it hadn't been cleaned.
   6 She won't be recognized in those dark glasses.

2 1 were caught, left/were leaving
   2 is … emptied
   3 have been granted

   4 were driving, were overtaken
   5 had been snowing
   6 arrive, 'll be picked up

5 1 1 moved
   2 have been living/have lived
   3 thought
   4 'll miss
   5 has been relocated
   6 didn't want
   7 'll have been
   8 has lived
   9 had … thought
   10 joined
   11 made
   12 've been learning
   13 don't like
   14 get
   15 's getting
   16 'll be able to
   17 misses
   18 don't live
   19 'll be
   20 'll … miss

2 1 How long has he lived/been living in Japan?
   2 Where did he move from?
   3 Why did he move there/to Japan?
   4 What did he do when he first arrived?
   5 What has he been studying for three years?
   6 Why doesn't he like writing Japanese?
   7 What does he miss most?
   8 When will he go back to Denver?

6 3 has (A)
   4 have (F)
   5 have (A)
   6 didn't (A)
   7 done (F)
   8 does (A)
   9 was (A)
   10 is (A)
   11 doing (F)
   12 did (F)

7 1 **A** have … got/do … have
  B 'm having
  B Have … got/Do … have
 2 **A** Have … got/Do … have
  B haven't/don't, Have/Do
  A 've had, 've got/have
  B to have
 3 **A** 've got/have
  B haven't got/don't have
  A had, Have
  B 've got/have
 4 **A** having, 've had, haven't had
  B haven't got/don't have

8 1 blood
 2 book
 3 water
 4 green
 5 night
 6 case
 7 bag
 8 rain
 9 sun
 10 road
 11 air
 12 day
 13 hand
 14 ice
 15 land
 16 card
 17 sports
 18 book

9 1 1 a 2 b 3 a 4 b 5 b 6 a

 2 1 brought home to me
 2 got on like a house on fire
 3 make yourselves at home
 4 brought the house down
 5 as safe as houses
 6 on the house

10 1 1 out
 2 away
 3 down
 4 off
 5 down/in
 6 off, on
 7 out
 8 back
 9 in
 10 away/out

 2 1 put … up (I), Put up (L)
 2 sorted out (L), sort … out (I)
 3 stand up (L), stand up (I)
 4 take … off (L), take off (I)
 5 picked … up (I), pick up (L)
 6 Hold on (I), hold on (L)

11 1 ✓ dad's chicken curry, ✓ friends from
  home, ✓ living in a house

 2 1 ✗ 2 ✗ 3 ✗ 4 ✓ 5 ✗ 6 ✗
  7 ✓

3 (I've) Just finished my first assignment
 (Do you) Fancy tea and cake in my
 room to celebrate?
 (I've) Always got time for cake.
 (I) Know what you mean.
 (It) Tastes yummy.
 (I) Thought it was just me.
 (I) Can't really do that here as our
 rooms are so small.
 Students aren't the tidiest (people in the
 world).
 (Do you) Want some more?

12 1 1 friend
 2 English
 3 clean
 4 month
 5 took
 6 news
 7 fans
 8 box
 9 thought
 10 work
 11 chart
 12 winter

 2

/e/	/ɪ/	/iː/	/ʌ/
letter	busy	freak	culprit
shelter	decide	sweeper	couple
dead	business	lethal	rough
/ʊ/	/uː/	/æ/	/ɒ/
woman	zoom	barrier	drop
should	drew	family	autobiography
goodness	suitable	accident	shock
/ɔː/	/ɜː/	/ɑː/	/ə/
water	birth	alarm	suspicious
abroad	earth	far	adopt
orphanage	Sir	father	beggar

Unit 2

1 1 He's written three magazine articles
  so far.
  He's been writing a travel blog since
  he left home.
 2 They've missed the bus again.
  They've been missing you lots, so
  come home soon.
 3 Paula's been leaving work early all
  this week.
  Paula's left work early to run some
  errands.
 4 I've lost my car keys.
  I've been losing weight recently.
 5 She's been talking on the phone for
  ages.
  She's talked about this subject before.
 6 The cat's been going next door to
  have its dinner.
  The cat's gone upstairs.

 7 He's had a heart attack.
  He's been having second thoughts
  about the job.
 8 I've been saving up to buy a brand
  new 52-inch TV.
  I've saved up about £500.
 9 I've been swimming, which is why
  my hair is wet.
  I've swum 20 lengths today.
 10 I've been finding it hard to
  concentrate recently.
  I've found my cheque book at last.

2 1 have climbed
 2 scaled
 3 have been dumping
 4 melts
 5 are turning
 6 have been working
 7 are now being shown
 8 was collected
 9 includes
 10 was looking
 11 had
 12 range
 13 will be going
 14 are trying

3 1 the 1700s
 2 were … known
 3 did, walk the tightrope
 4 happened, all fell off the tightrope
  and survived
 5 have, been known as, Since
 6 How old was, fell
 7 was, born, in 1979

4 1 1 becomes
 2 has been trying
 3 has been granted
 4 holds
 5 started
 6 have been spraying
 7 has been blasted
 8 We're playing
 9 will be traversing
 10 will be suspended
 11 feels
 12 didn't want
 13 are broadcasting
 14 being shown

 2 2 has been performing, performed
 3 'm having, 've had
 4 are you thinking, think
 5 was banging, 've … banged
 6 've been reading, read
 7 fought, Have you been fighting
 8 'm expecting, expect
 9 is being decorated, is decorated
 10 be losing, has lost

5 1 2 Have the street lights been repaired yet?
3 Some new anti-drug laws have just been passed.
4 No new homes have been built for 20 years.
5 The plants haven't been watered.

2 2 Bankers' bonuses have been slashed.
3 Fishermen have been rescued dramatically in the Pacific Ocean.
4 Over 400 people have been killed in the monsoon in Pakistan.
5 Dali painting has been stolen in New York.
6 Ancient pyramids have been discovered in Sudan.
7 A missing teenager has been found alive.
8 Four hundred and sixty-four jobs have been axed in a shock announcement by the Council.

6 1 2 have her ears pierced
3 have my eyes tested
4 have had their car serviced
5 had our television repaired yet

2 Recently …
She's had the wedding dress made.
They've had the cake decorated.
Yesterday …
They had the champagne delivered.
He had his hair cut.
Today …
She's having her hair styled.
They're having the flowers delivered.
Next week …
They'll have had the photos developed.
They'll have had her wedding dress and his suit dry-cleaned.

7 1 a tour operator
b Ecuadorian Amazon
c travel writer
d Vienna
e film director
f the Navajo Nation

2 1 VS 2 GB 3 KM 4 KM 5 GB
6 VS

3 1 ✓ 2 ✗ 3 ✗ 4 ✓ 5 ✗ 6 ✗

4 **stunning** views/destination/places/hotel
friendly atmosphere/welcome/places/hotel/
romantic fire/views/haunt/destination/places/hotel/atmosphere
enchanting views/haunt/destination/places/hotel/atmosphere
adventurous tourist
sunlit terrace
crackling fire
interesting destination/places/hotel/alternatives

enthusiastic welcome
five-star hotel
perfect views/haunt/destination/hotel/atmosphere

8 1

	car	bus	bike	train	plane	ship/ferry
get into/out of	✓					
get on/off		✓	✓	✓	✓	✓
take off					✓	
land					✓	
ride			✓			
drive	✓	✓		✓		
catch		✓		✓	✓	✓
miss		✓		✓	✓	✓
board		✓		✓	✓	✓
park	✓	✓				

2 **car:** traffic lights, one-way street, Customs, traffic warden, horn, seat belt, service station, tyres, traffic jam
bus: traffic lights, one-way street, horn, season ticket, timetable, deck, ticket inspector, tyres, traffic jam
bike: helmet, traffic lights, one-way street, tyres, cycle lane
train: season ticket, track, baggage rack, Customs, platform, trolley, horn, timetable, aisle/window seat, ticket inspector, carriage
plane: runway, Customs, security check, life jacket, trolley, check-in desk, timetable, aisle/window seat, tyres, hand luggage, overhead locker
ship/ferry: Customs, cabin, harbour, life jacket, trolley, horn, timetable, deck, port

9 1 at
2 out of
3 across/into/to
4 to
5 through
6 towards
7 off
8 onto
9 over
10 into
11 past/through
12 to
13 into
14 against/on
15 in
16 out of
17 along
18 past
19 across
20 over
21 up/along
22 onto

10 1 1 explorer, exploration
2 politics, politician
3 photograph, photographer
4 luxury, luxurious
5 produce, production
6 Japan, Japanese

2, 3

●● ●	● ● ● ●	● ● ●
produce Japan success reject pollute complain	explorer production instructor authentic illegal	politics photograph luxury paradise scientists backpacker infinite Philippines packaging charity
●● ●	● ● ● ●	● ● ● ●
Japanese afternoon Bangladesh	exploration politician disappointment destination European	photographer luxurious adrenaline spectacular memorial community Cambodia emergency

Unit 3

1 2 saved
3 had been
4 came through
5 was drowning
6 had arrived
7 had been bodyboarding
8 swept
9 had seen
10 swam
11 had managed
12 was struggling
13 hovered
14 was lowered
15 was airlifted
16 made
17 were

2 1,2 1 stuck ✓
2 had stuck ✓
3 fell ✗
4 had fallen ✗
5 cost ✓
6 had cost ✓
7 had never flown ✗
8 flew ✗
9 had caught ✓
10 caught ✓
11 were ✗
12 had been ✗

3
1. was living, met
2. played, were winning, lost
3. wasn't thinking, had
4. was coughing, didn't get
5. was snowing, got up, were making, put, raced
6. was playing, hit, made
7. happened, was walking, noticed, wanted, vanished
8. was sunbathing, heard, appeared, landed

4 1 2 a 3 c 4 b 5 o 6 h 7 e
8 f 9 i 10 g 11 l 12 m 13 n
14 k 15 j

2 1 Two years ago, while I was working in Paris, my grandfather died.
2 As soon as I got home, I switched on the TV.
3 First I had a shower and then I got dressed.
4 Since I was a child, I had always wanted to visit Australia, and I finally went last year.
5 As he posted the letter, he realized that he hadn't put a stamp on it.
6 By the time he'd finished speaking, most of the audience had fallen asleep.
7 Once I'd told him the truth, I felt better.
8 Until I found a flat, I had stayed/been staying with friends for months.

5
2. A Roman temple was discovered underneath the new housing estate.
3. The races were held indoors because it was raining.
4. The swimming pool had been booked for a children's party on Saturday afternoon.
5. The dishwasher was being repaired, so I couldn't leave the house.
6. Our hotel room still hadn't been cleaned when we returned.
7. The fish hadn't been cooked for long enough.
8. New traffic lights were being put up at the crossroads.

6
1. saw
2. was … shown/released
3. were adored
4. has released
5. combines
6. are taken
7. worked
8. are studying
9. loathe
10. tells
11. overcome
12. become

13. directed
14. composed
15. has … made
16. has achieved
17. has come
18. will find

7 plot **T**, **B**; storyline **B**; chapter **B**; stalls **T**; critic **F**, **T**, **B**; director **F**, **T**; backstage **T**; trailer **F**; script **F**, **T**; rehearsal **T**; review **F**, **T**, **B**; e-reader **B**; character **F**, **T**, **B**; musical **F**, **T**; starring role **F**, **T**; novelist **B**; matinee **T**; prequel/sequel **F**; documentary **F**; blockbuster **F**, **B**; animation **F**; screen **F**; interval **T**; fairy tale **F**; programme **T**; whodunnit **B**; science fiction **F**, **B**; hardback **B**; dressing-room **T**; performance **F**, **T**; thriller **F**, **B**; playwright **T**; autobiography **B**; full house **T**; paperback **B**

8 1 2 i 3 b 4 g 5 j 6 h 7 a 8 f
9 e 10 c

2 1 turns up
2 setting off
3 Cheer up
4 stay in
5 settled down
6 broke up
7 find out
8 Shut up
9 Speak up
10 Hold on

9 1 1 had a relaxing afternoon
2 an article she read
3 Alec Baldwin
4 his ex-wife
5 the same
6 an acrimonious
7 dating

2 1 b 2 c 3 e 4 a 5 f 6 d

10 1 1 pay /peɪ/
2 write /raɪt/
3 phone /fəʊn/
4 round /raʊnd/
5 dear /dɪə/
6 boy /bɔɪ/
7 tour /tʊə/
8 fair /feə/

2 3 /əʊ/   4 /uː/
5 /ɔː/   6 /ɜː/
7 /ɪə/   8 /ɜː/
9 /ɔː/   10 /ɜː/
11 /aʊ/   12 /əʊ/
13 /uː/   14 /əʊ/
15 /əʊz/   16 /əʊs/   17 /uːz/
18 /uːs/   19 /uːz/
20 /əʊm/   21 /uːm/   22 /ɒm/
23 /ɒl/   24 /əʊl/
25 /əʊm/   26 /ʌm/

27 /eɪ/   28 /eɪ/
29 /eɪ/   30 /e/
31 /ʌ/   32 /uː/   33 /ʊ/
34 /əʊld/ 35 /ʊd/
36 /ʌ/   37 /ɒ/   38 /əʊ/

Unit 4

1
2. How long
3. Who made/directed the film 'Catch Me If You Can'?
4. How old was Frank when his parents
5. What was his first major con?
6. Which … did he
7. Where did he impersonate
8. Why did he (decide to) change course?
9. What did he teach (when he was a university professor)?
10. Where was he arrested?
11. Who starred as/played Frank in the movie/film ('Catch Me If You Can')?
12. Who does Frank work for now?/ Where does Frank work now?

2 1 2 how he learned to forge cheques
3 why his parents divorced
4 who decided to make a musical
5 which countries he visited
6 how he had the nerve to impersonate a doctor
7 why the police took so long to catch him
8 how he got the job with the FBI

2 1 how much money he made
2 what the film is called/what the title of the film is/what the name of the film is
3 which airline he flew for
4 who starred in the film ('Catch Me If You Can')
5 is working/works for the FBI?

3 1 2 by
3 to
4 at
5 on
6 in
7 about
8 of
9 with
10 from

2 2 What for?
3 Where to?
4 What about?
5 How long for?
6 Who for?
7 Who to?
8 What with?

4 1 don't
2 didn't
3 haven't

4 aren't
5 isn't
6 won't
7 'm not
8 doesn't
9 hadn't
10 hasn't
11 wasn't
12 weren't

5 1 a 2 b 3 c 4 d 5 f 6 e
    7 g 8 h 9 j 10 i

6 1 not
    2 no
    3 None
    4 not
    5 not
    6 n't
    7 not
    8 not
    9 no
    10 Not
    11 none
    12 no
    13 n't
    14 not
    15 Not
    16 none
    17 no
    18 no
    19 None
    20 Not

7 2 I don't suppose you've got change for a 20-euro note.
    3 This machine doesn't seem to be working.
    4 I didn't think it was going to rain.
    5 They don't want their daughter to move to Canada.
    6 I didn't expect to see you here.
    7 I don't suppose you've seen Robert recently.
    8 I don't think I'd like snails.
    9 I don't expect you remember me.
    10 I don't believe she passed all her exams.

8 1 1 E 2 C 3 H 4 A 5 D 6 G
       7 F 8 B

    2 2 C 3 A 4 E 5 D 6 B 7 F
       8 G

9 2 for
    3 of/from
    4 from
    5 in
    6 to
    7 in
    8 in
    9 to/with
    10 to, about
    11 at

12 in, with
13 for
14 in

10 1, 2

Adjectives	
untruthful	dishonest
incredible	unbelievable
implausible	ridiculous
improbable	unlikely
displeased	annoyed
abnormal	bizarre
unprofessional	amateur
unimportant	trivial
Nouns	
dishonesty	deceit
unreality	fantasy
disbelief	incredulity
Verbs	
disappear	vanish
misunderstand	confuse
mistrust/distrust	suspect
uncover	reveal

11 1 2 aren't you (fall)
       3 wasn't it (fall)
       4 couldn't you (fall)
       5 isn't he (fall)
       6 isn't it (fall)
       7 did he (rise)
       8 have you (fall)
       9 weren't we (rise)
       10 would you (fall)

    2 2 That was a really tasteless meal, wasn't it? (fall)
       3 You've borrowed my new coat again, haven't you? (fall)
       4 You couldn't/wouldn't water my plants, could/would you? (rise)
       5 Vanessa, you're going on a business trip to Rome, aren't you? (rise)

Unit 5

1 1 You're going to work harder from now on, aren't you?
    2 I'll see you next week, won't I?
    3 Kate's leaving soon, isn't she?
    4 You'll ring when you get there, won't you?
    5 Our plane takes off at 4 p.m., doesn't it?
    6 The painters will have finished by next week, won't they?
    7 You aren't getting married next week, are you?
    8 We won't need tickets to get in, will we?
    9 We'll be millionaires one day, won't we?
    10 Max won't be coming, will he?

2 1 'm going to, 'll
    2 are going to, 'll
    3 'm going to, 'll, 'll
    4 will/is going to, 'll
    5 's going to, 'll
    6 'll/'m going to, 'm going to, 'll
    7 'm going to, 'll
    8 'll, 'll

3 2 I'll buy her a present.
    3 I'm going to study hard for my exams.
    4 I'm seeing/going to see the dentist next Friday.
    5 I think Manchester United will win on Saturday.
    6 I'm going to be late for the meeting.
    7 My sister is expecting/having a baby in March.
    8 My plane leaves at 7.30 a.m. (from London, Heathrow).
    9 This time next week I'll be lying on a beach in Spain.
    10 I think it'll be hot there.

4 1 work in the US (**J**); live in the north of England (**M**); move to London (**T**); travel the world (**T**); study law (**J**); buy a farm (**M**); win an Olympic medal (**M**); mix with celebrities (**J**); design swimwear (**M**); marry a film star (**J**); live near the river (**T**); buy a penthouse flat (**T**); go clubbing and partying (**J**)

    2 *Sample answers:*
       By the time Tommy is 30, …
       3 he'll have bought a penthouse flat.
       4 he'll be living near the River Thames.
       5 he'll have travelled all over the world.

       By the time Jack is 30, …
       1 he'll have become a lawyer (for one of the best firms) in New York.
       2 he'll be mixing with celebrities.
       3 he'll have married a (rich) film star.
       4 he'll be going clubbing and partying.

       By the time Millie is 30, she …
       1 she'll be living in the north of England/the Lake District.
       2 she'll have won an Olympic medal.
       3 she'll have bought a farm.
       4 she'll have designed her own brand of swimwear.

5 1 'm taking
    2 'm going to be
    3 'll be hoping
    4 'll never give up
    5 win
    6 'll have been training
    7 are being staged
    8 'll have concentrated
    9 will be

10 be hoping
11 will
12 will be

6 1 eat, won't get
2 won't move, 've found
3 'll love, meet
4 Will/Are … going to … learn, 're
5 won't go, have/have had
6 'll be, finish/'ve finished
7 don't do, will … have to
8 are, will deal
9 'll feel, 've had
10 've tried, 'll never use

7 2 **A** What are you doing/going to do
B ✓
3 **A** ✓
B What am I going to do?
4 **A** is going to the States
B ✓
5 **A** ✓
B You'll have to wake me up.
6 **A** ✓
B You'll be getting
7 **A** ✓
B It'll only take
8 **A** ✓
B We're going to stay at home.
9 **A** as soon as I arrive
B ✓
10 **A** ✓
B unless I get held up

8 1 taking
2 puts
3 putting
4 took
5 took
6 take
7 take
8 put
9 put
10 taken
11 put
12 take

9 1 a 're waiting for
b is expected
c looking forward to
2 a spend/'ve been spending/'ve
spent/'m spending
b pass
c wasted
3 a Have … seen
b watched/were watching
c Look at
4 a Actually
b at the moment
c really
5 a owe
b borrowed
c lend

6 a embarrassed
b nervous
c angry

10 3 I couldn't take them all in.
4 I'll sort it out tomorrow.
5 Put it in your diary.
6 Please put them away.
7 … you'd better look after him.
8 I'll look into it right away.
9 Take it back!
10 … you've put me off her.

11 1 1 won't /əʊ/
2 walk /ɔː/
3 wonder /ʌ/
4 woman /ʊ/
5 warm /ɔː/
6 word /ɜː/
7 wear /eə/
8 weight /eɪ/
9 want /ɒ/
10 work /ɜː/
11 wander /ɒ/
12 women /ɪ/
13 worm /ɜː/
14 ward /ɔː/
15 weary /ɪə/
16 weird /ɪə/

2 1 phone /əʊ/
2 blood /ʌ/
3 love /ʌ/
4 through /uː/
5 weak /iː/
6 lower /əʊ/
7 north /ɔː/
8 height /aɪ/
9 pear /eə/
10 hear /ɪə/

Unit 6

1 1 cash
2 unemployment
3 traffic
4 luggage
5 food
6 music
7 violence
8 opportunity
9 ingredient
10 fluid

2 1 some, any
2 Some, any
3 some, any
4 any, any
5 some, some
6 any

3 2 Is there much work to be done in the
garden?
3 I didn't spend much time on the
homework.

4 Did they do much research before
they found a cure?
5 I didn't have too many problems with
this exercise either.
6 I've got too much luggage. I can't
carry it all.
7 There is too much traffic on the
streets of our town.
8 They couldn't give me much
information about the delay to our
flight.

4 1 *Sample answers:*
1 There are lots of cheese sandwiches.
2 There are a few chocolate biscuits.
3 There's a little vegetable curry and
rice.
4 There isn't much rice or fruit salad.
5 There's a huge amount of spaghetti.
6 There are several hamburgers.
7 There are no chips or chocolate cake.
8 There aren't many tuna sandwiches.
9 There are a couple of doughnuts.
10 There's hardly any apple juice.

2 3 lots
4 a few
5 not much/hardly any
6 n't any/none
7 a little
8 a few
9 a little
10 some/a few
11 a couple of, lots/a huge amount

5 2 a few, a little
3 have less … than
4 few/very few
5 a little
6 Fewer
7 Few
8 a few
9 is … little
10 a few

6 1 1 somewhere
2 anyone/anybody
3 anywhere
4 anything
5 everything
6 nothing
7 Nobody/No one
8 nowhere
9 someone/somebody
10 something, anything
11 anyone/anybody
12 Everyone/Everybody

2 1 b 2 a 3 c 4 d 5 f 6 e
7 h 8 g 9 i 10 j 11 l 12 k
13 m 14 n 15 o 16 p

7 1 many
2 a bit
3 few